AIN'T NO RAG

AIN'T NO RAG

FREEDOM, FAMILY, AND THE FLAG

Charlie Daniels

Since 1947
REGNERY
PUBLISHING, INC.
An Eagle Publishing Company • Washington, DC

Library of Congress Cataloging-in-Publication Data on file with the Library of Congress

Published in the United States by
Regnery Publishing, Inc.
An Eagle Publishing Company
One Massachusetts Avenue, NW
Washington, DC 20001

Visit us at www.regnery.com

Distributed to the trade by
National Book Network
4720-A Boston Way
Lanham, MD 20706

Printed on acid-free paper

Manufactured in the United States of America

10 9 8 7 6 5 4 3 2 1

Books are available in quantity for promotional or premium use. Write to Director of Special Sales, Regnery Publishing, Inc., One Massachusetts Avenue, NW, Washington, DC 20001, for information on discounts and terms or call (202) 216-0600.

Family *is the cornerstone of stability and I dedicate this work to my wife, Hazel, and my son, Charlie, and thank God for the anchor they have been in my life.* ♪

CONTENTS

PART TWO: WHY I LOVE AMERICA

PART THREE: FAITH AND FAMILY

IN AMERICA

I have not been a successful musician all my life. I know what it's like to get up before the sun does and work until it's going down again. I know what it's like to try to stretch a paycheck from the first till the fifteenth. I know about rent and car payments, patched jeans and thin-soled shoes.

The first house I remember living in had electricity but no running water. Did you ever take a bath in a galvanized washtub on a cold night? The side toward the fire is burning up and the side away from the fire is freezing. You're red on one side and blue on the other.

Our sanitary facility was a short walk from the back door, and yes, folks, it's true; the Sears & Roebuck catalog did spend its dotage in the little house behind the big house growing thinner by the day and titillating the imagination of little boys who sat there ogling the scantily clad models in the lingerie section.

We seldom locked our doors and I can remember a time when I didn't know anybody at all who didn't believe in God.

If you didn't have a job you were looking for one, and the work ethic of the day was a day's work for a day's pay. Your job security was just how well you did the job. At that time unions were pretty much nonexistent in our little corner of the world.

Almost everybody owned at least one gun, usually a rifle or a shotgun, and all the males in my family were hunters. I was taught gun safety at a very early age, and I would have no more thought about bothering with a gun than I would have thought about picking up a snake. I just knew better.

"Spare the rod and spoil the child" was very much in effect at my house. My mother could wield a switch with the dexterity of an Olympic fencer and meted out the corporeal punishment in accordance with the offense, and as the old saying goes I never got a lick amiss. I'm thankful that my parents loved me enough to teach me right from wrong and respect for people and property.

Humble, yes, but treasured memories all, and I'll never "get above my raising," as they used to say down in North Carolina.

So if my writing strikes you as rural, I came by it honestly and make absolutely no apologies.

My Soapbox

One of the most precious things guaranteed under our Constitution is freedom of speech, which means freedom of opinion and the lawful right to voice that opinion in any forum we choose.

Pro or con, right or wrong, simple or eloquent, we have the right to tell the world what we think about politics, personalities, or the price of peanut butter. I ardently believe in expressing my opinion and I wish that everybody would do the same.

When I started doing the soapbox article several years ago for our website, www.charliedaniels.com, what I wanted was a forum for my thoughts and the means by which my readers could respond and let me know what they thought about what I had written.

My soapbox columns, many of them collected in this volume and left pretty much the way they appeared on our website when I wrote them, are not an attempt to ram my ideas down the collective throat of America. They are simply my personal thoughts on a variety of subjects which range from the serious to the ridiculous.

I have found that many things have more than just two sides. Sometimes the ramifications of an issue can affect so many people in so many different ways.

For the most part I speak and write in the vernacular of the street from whence I came. I lay no claim to great wisdom and I barely made it through the twelfth grade. My education comes not from the world of academia but from exposure and experience.

Sometimes my subjects are as bland as beeswax and sometimes as hot as Cajun pepper sauce. One time I may write a poem or an essay on some place I think is beautiful and the next on a current event I feel strongly about.

Through my writings I have found many kindred spirits and some not so kindred who hate what I write so badly that all they can do is expound a string of expletives that would make a rodeo cowboy put his hands over his face.

In my time I have had it out with actors, newspaper people, television producers, talk show hosts, and a vast assortment of doctors, lawyers, and Indian chiefs who have called me anything from a pretty good sort of feller to a warmongering SOB.

For example, much has been made of a soapbox piece I wrote called "An Open Letter to the Hollywood Bunch," in which I chided some actors, in no uncertain terms, about their tasteless war protests. I don't deny anybody's right to say anything they want to and to protest anything they so desire.

But when you go to Iraq as Sean Penn did, and compare the commander in chief with Hitler as David Clennon did, I think you're going way beyond the pale. Their protests were actually not as much antiwar as a thinly disguised anti-Bush campaign. I never heard a word out of them when Clinton sent missiles flying.

Another example of controversy took place in the summer of 2002, when my band was asked to be a part of a PBS Fourth of

July television production called *A Capitol Fourth*. It is a show which has been going on for many years, takes place in Washington, D.C., in front of a tremendous crowd, and all in all is quite a prestigious thing to appear on.

When we submitted the songs we wanted to perform, we sent a song I had just written called "The Last Fallen Hero," which dealt with the 9-11 tragedy. I felt it was one of the most fitting songs we had for a Fourth of July celebration in the nation's capital.

We received word from the producer that we could not do that song on his show. His reasoning was that this was to be a happy, hot dogs and watermelon, fireworks, grand old flag kind of affair and that any mention of 9-11 would be too morbid.

I pulled out of the show not because of any star trip or ego. I felt that it would be tantamount to being un-American to celebrate the first birthday of this nation after 9-11 and not devote at least three minutes to the memory of the innocent and brave people who died that day.

So when we received word from Atlanta, Georgia, "Tell Charlie to come on down here and play for our Fourth of July celebration and he can play anything he wants to," we took Atlanta up on its offer. I may never understand some of the people in Washington.

You will find that my sympathies and concerns lie mainly with the blue collar crowd. That's where I came from and where my heart will always be. I have strong convictions about the things I write about and if they happen to go against the popular thinking *du jour*, that's just too bad.

I take on some pretty divisive subjects in this book: war, gun control, abortion, NAFTA, the United Nations, and a myriad of other issues which have many critics and many defenders. But my opinion is not shaped by what somebody else thinks. It is a byproduct of my own reflection and gut reaction, and I have not the least bit of timidity in letting you know what it is. For example:

- I hate political correctness. I think it's silly and I will not yield an inch to it wherever it raises its frivolous head. In my mind, touchy feely, *I'm OK you're OK, ain't we wonderful*–type blather is nothing more than a substance I can dig up in my barnyard. And I raise bulls.

- I believe that too many people go into marriage these days without the commitment it takes to make it successful. I believe that some people take the very serious act of bringing children into this world much too lightly.
- I believe that anyone who fathers a child should be responsible for that child's support until it reaches the age of majority and that if the father does not furnish that support he should go to jail.
- Too many children are left to run the streets by parents whose only interest in them is the monthly welfare check. I believe in welfare but only for those who truly need it. The rest should work for a living.
- Political double talk is another one of my pet peeves. I just hate it when some hotshot politico answers a question with another question. I guess you just have to learn to translate politispeak into plain English. For instance:

Politispeak: "Well, Senator, what have you got to say about voting against the pay raise for the military?"

"Well, John, you know I support our men and women in uniform but this administration is just going about this the wrong way."

Plain English: "My party didn't come up with this bill and I'm afraid it will make the other party look good so I'm not about to vote for it."

Politispeak: "Senator, why are you against the tax cut?"

"This country can't afford a tax cut at this time; it will ruin the economy and eliminate jobs."

Plain English: "Are you kidding? Give money back to the citizens? They may learn that they do a better job of spending it than we do, and besides it may endanger one of my pork barrel projects."

You get the idea.

Politicians are a different breed. I sometimes think that there is a kind of sickness that exists only inside the Washington Beltway. When these people leave home their eyes are full of stars and their mouths are full of promises, but once inside the Beltway it seems that everything changes and most of them are content to just toe the party line.

I am a big supporter of term limits. I believe that our political process was designed for someone to serve a couple of terms and then go home and let someone fresh off the streets come on board. Someone who is in touch with what is going on in the real world now. Someone who can relate to the needs of the people firsthand.

I feel that politicians who stay in Washington too long form acquaintances and alliances that tend to allow them to gather way too much power and influence around themselves.

I know that the common argument against term limits is that we can vote them out, but I can't vote out the senator from another state who has been in office for twenty-five years and delivers so much pork to his state that his constituency will never vote him out. If any company in this nation was operated like the federal government, it would be out of business within a year. It's easy to spend somebody else's money, and that's our money they're spending.

Common Sense Through My Eyes

I have a simplistic way of looking at things. I use what I call "cowboy logic." It goes like this: two and two is always four, water never runs uphill, and if there is smoke there is a fire somewhere.

- If 70 percent or so of our crime is caused by drugs, why aren't we spending 70 percent of our law enforcement budget on doing away with them?
- If the United Nations has proven to be so ineffective and anti-American, why don't we just resign and let them move the UN building to France or somewhere and stop spending our hard-earned money on it?
- In the world of international politics, why don't we call a friend a friend and an enemy an enemy? Semantics are not going to change facts.
- If some people are so dead set against their children hearing the name of God or saying the Pledge of Allegiance in school, why don't we just give parents school vouchers so they can send their children to the schools of their own choosing? Then their children would only be exposed to the ideas they want them exposed to.
- If we expect the men and women in our military and the police who patrol our streets to lay their lives on the line for us, why aren't they better paid?
- Why do we keep giving cash to other nations to supposedly feed their starving populations? Why not just cut out the middle man and send food? I'm sure our farmers would be glad about that.
- Why do we scream for more gun control and ignore the fact that never in the history of man has a gun ever gone out and shot somebody without a finger pulling the trigger? You have to control the finger, not the gun.
- Why do we stand so firmly against giving the death sentence to some wanton killer and not say a word about the death sentence given to innocent unborn babies by wholesale abortion?
- Why do we have to be Native Americans or African Americans? Can't we just all be Americans, color of skin and

heritage notwithstanding? Isn't that what we've fought for all these years?

- Why do antiwar protestors always seem to forget that the reason they enjoy the right to protest is because Americans fought and won so many wars?

No One Likes War, But...

War is a horrible thing, always nasty, but sometimes necessary. My first recollections of war began on December the 7th, 1941, with the Japanese sneak attack on Pearl Harbor. The news fell like a ton of bricks on the shoulders of a nation already concerned about sending its sons to Europe to confront Hitler.

President Roosevelt said that December 7, 1941, would be a day that would live in infamy. Well, it was also the day that America got her back up. The war effort was on and I can tell you that watching this country operate at 100 percent is an awesome sight to see.

The grown folks volunteered for the military and the kids collected scrap metal. Everybody was involved in some way.

The war was very real in our part of the country. Wilmington, North Carolina, is a seaport town and was the home of a shipyard during the war years. German U-boats lay off our coast to sink the oil tankers which left our ports bound for Europe. Slogans like "Loose Lips Sink Ships" were very prominently displayed and adhered to.

The Hollywood stars of that day appeared at bond rallies and USO shows. Some of them even joined up for active military service. Now that's a change, ain't it?

The cruelty of Hitler's Nazi regime came home to us in the stark black and white newsreel pictures as we watched the naked, skeletal bodies of dead Jews being pushed into mass graves by bulldozers like so much garbage.

The lessons I learned from that war are many. I learned that there is evil in the world that sometimes manifests itself in a cruelty which is beyond the understanding of civilized people. I learned that that kind of cruelty cannot be tolerated. It has to be destroyed.

It cannot be contained, nor placated, and no amount of diplomacy will make the slightest dent in it. Nothing short of total destruction will get the job done. We should have learned that lesson well with the first Gulf War.

America's Worth Fighting For

I believe fervently in the American Dream and I myself am a prime example of its validity today. I believe that everybody has a chance to be somebody in this country. It doesn't come easy and the price is not cheap. It takes a fire in the belly and the burning of the midnight oil, the willingness to be the first one to get there and the last one to leave, the will to work twice as hard as everybody else if that's what it takes.

There are a few absolutes in achieving success but there is no yellow brick road. Everybody has to find their own way in their own time. Success is pyramid shaped; there is plenty of room at the bottom but the closer you get to the top, the narrower it becomes, and only the most highly motivated venture there.

There is no such thing as luck; you make your own luck. Nothing can be left to chance; there is only hard work and the blessings of God.

The American Dream lives. If a nominally talented, chubby, nearsighted kid from North Carolina can make it, you can too.

In 1958, I left small-town, rural America and walked out into a world I knew very little about to seek my fortune in the entertainment business, a business which has taken me from the 38th Parallel to the Eiffel Tower, from the Mediterranean to the polar ice cap. I've sat around cowboy cook fires in the middle of nowhere and walked the teeming streets of Hong Kong. There's hardly a major highway in this nation I haven't traversed and I've kept twenty-five people steadily and gainfully employed for almost thirty years.

I say this not to boast—far from it—but to emphasize where I'm coming from. God has indeed been good to me. He gave me the salvation of His Son, Jesus Christ, and a life I could only dream about all those years ago in Carolina.

Some of my pieces may amuse you, others may provoke you. Some may stir up nostalgia or a long-forgotten pleasant memory.

Whatever your reaction, I hope you'll enjoy this collection of thoughts and I hope they will encourage you to let your opinion be known.

PART 1

COWBOY LOGIC

If you don't like
the way I'm living,
just leave this long-haired
country boy alone.

—"Long-Haired Country Boy,"
from Fire on the Mountain, 1974

JUST TO LET YOU KNOW

Some of you folks out there are probably wondering why we didn't appear on the CMT Country Freedom Concert for the Salvation Army to benefit the victims of the September 11th attack on America.

We were announced and scheduled and had every intention of doing the show, until we gave the CMT folks the lyrics to a new song I had written and wanted to perform on the show.

After receiving the words they informed us that we could not do the song on the show and when we asked them why, they said that the show was a healing type show and they were afraid that the song would offend someone.

I would never do anything to hurt the show but I knew that they had the very epitome of country stars and didn't particularly need us to sell tickets.

With this in mind, I decided to pull off the show for personal reasons which I would like to share with you.

Let me preface my remarks by saying that I respect CMT's right to not allow anything they don't agree with to go out over their airwaves. And in all fairness, I guess they were taking the sensibilities of the victim's families into account. But I respectfully and vehemently disagree with their stand.

First of all, I don't feel that this is the time for healing. I feel that this is the time to rub salt in the wounds and keep America focused on the job at hand.

We lost almost three thousand people in the Twin Towers and Pentagon and we're worrying about offending somebody?

We have seven-month-old babies infected with anthrax and we're afraid we'll hurt someone's feelings?

Brave Americans forced a plane down in a field in Pennsylvania and we're worried about ruffling someone's feathers?

We're sending our sons and daughters off to fight and perhaps die in a war we had nothing to do with starting and we're concerned about insulting somebody?

I felt to give in to this political correctness would be to turn my back on the people who lost their lives on 9-11 and on the brave men and women who defend this country.

The title of the song is "This Ain't No Rag; It's a Flag," and I don't apologize for a word in it. I'll let you all decide for yourselves:

This ain't no rag; it's a flag, and we don't wear it on our heads
It's a symbol of the land where the good guys live; are you listening to what I said?
You're a coward and a fool and you broke all the rules and you wounded our American pride
Now we're coming with a gun and we know you're gonna run but you can't find no place to hide
We're gonna hunt you down like a mad dog hound and make you pay for the lives you stole
We're all through talking and messing around and now it's time to rock and roll
These colors don't run and we're speaking as one when we say united we stand
If you mess with one you mess with us all, every boy, girl, woman and man
You've been acting mighty rash and talking that trash but let me give you some advice
You can crawl back in your hole like a dirty little mole but now it's time to pay the price

You might have shot us in the back but now you have to face the fact that the big boy's in the game

The lightning's been flashing and the thunder's been crashing and now it's gettin' ready to rain

CHORUS:

This is the United States of America, the land of the brave and free

We believe in God, we believe in justice, we believe in liberty

You've been pulling our chain; we should'a done something about you a long time ago

But now the flag's flying high and the fur's gonna fly and now the whole world's gonna know

This ain't no rag; it's a flag, old glory red white and blue, the stars and stripes

And when it comes to a fight, we can do what we have to do

Our people stand proud, the American crowd is faithful and loyal and tough

We're as good as the best and better than the rest; you're gonna find out soon enough

When you look up in the sky and you see the eagle fly you'd better know he's headed your way

This ain't no rag; it's a flag, and it stands for the U.S.A.

OPEN LETTER TO PBS

Below are the lyrics to a new song we recently recorded and had intended to do on the "Capitol Fourth" television show, which is broadcast live from the Mall in Washington, D.C., on the Fourth of July, 2002:

"THE LAST FALLEN HERO"

The cowards came by morning
And attacked without a warning
Leaving death and flames and chaos in our streets
And in the middle of this fiery hell
Brave heroes fell
In the skies of Pennsylvania
On a plane bound for destruction
With the devil and his angels at the wheel
They never reached their target on the ground
Brave heroes brought it down

CHORUS:
This is a righteous cause
So without doubt or pause
I will do what my country asks of me
Make any sacrifice
We'll pay whatever price
So the children of tomorrow can be free

Lead on red, white, and blue
And we will follow you
Until we win the final victory
God help us do our best
We will not slack nor rest
Till the last fallen hero rests in peace
Oh the winds of war are blowing
And there's no way of knowing
Where this bloody path we're traveling will lead
But we must follow to the end
Or face it all again
Make no mistake about it, write it, sing it, talk it, shout it
Across the mountains and the deserts and the seas
The blood of innocence and shame
Will not be shed in vain
REPEAT CHORUS

Below is the open letter to Jerry Colbert, producer of "A Capitol Fourth," the Fourth of July show on PBS:

"Mr. Colbert, I was honored and pleased when we were asked to be a part of your show and totally surprised at your reaction to 'The Last Fallen Hero.'

"We were informed by the powers that be at PBS, which I am assuming is you, Mr. Colbert, that we could not do the song on the show and I have respectfully declined to be on the show. We have recently gone through this same thing with another song named 'This Ain't No Rag, It's a Flag,' and I just don't want anybody to get the idea that I am on a star trip or being egotistical or petulant.

"Please let me explain. This song is a tribute to the people who lost their lives on 9-11, the policemen, firemen, and other emergency services people who paid the ultimate price in the service of their fellow man. The brave passengers who brought

down that ill-fated plane in the Pennsylvania countryside, the military personnel who were killed at the Pentagon, and the thousands of innocent people who lost their lives in the bombing of the Trade Towers.

"What better day to pay tribute to these fallen heroes than the Fourth of July? After all, what are we celebrating on Independence Day? We are celebrating the coming of age of the United States of America. The colors of the very flag we salute represent the sacrifices of brave men and women, the red representing the blood which was shed that we might have an Independence Day to celebrate.

"When I think of the young men and women who give up a goodly portion of their prime years to wear the uniform of this country and go off to stand in harm's way for a nation which is too politically correct to even acknowledge the war they're fighting on the Fourth of July, it makes me ashamed. I truly don't understand the actions of PBS, the network which espouses the causes of some pretty far-out characters in the name of freedom of speech. What happened to my freedom of speech? Is music excluded?

"I have made a living entertaining the public for over forty years now, and I think I have a pretty good idea of the national mood, and I assure you that this song would offend no one except the deplorable characters who attacked our nation.

"I thought the song was the perfect Fourth of July song and still do for that matter, and I assure we will be doing it for an appreciative audience in Atlanta, Georgia on the Fourth of July.

"I will not spend a Fourth of July at a place where I can't commend and encourage our military, and I will not turn my back even for a day on the thousands of innocent victims of 9-11. It is my feeling that they all deserve to be remembered on the birthday of the nation they died for.

"God Bless America,

"Charlie Daniels"

BAGHDAD SEAN IS AT IT AGAIN

There is a very radical, far left, little known satellite network which I will not even name, one of those condescending, pseudo-highbrow supposedly intellectual outfits that just love to criticize America.

I was surfing the other day and saw the face of none other than Baghdad Sean Penn, the traitorous little Hollywood hotshot who went to Iraq to try to make America look bad.

He was pointing out that the Iraqi people were in terrible shape, they were being deprived of the essentials of life, food and medicine and such, and that the American embargo was the cause of all their ills.

I got so mad I had to change channels. Here is this American citizen, who has reaped rewards far beyond those of 99.9 percent of the people in this nation, standing there blaming the woes of the Iraqi people on the United States of America.

This is idiocy. Our embargoes have caused this situation? Mr. Penn, did Saddam Hussein have nothing to do with it?

Do you not think that this unspeakable monster and his family live in mansions and indulge their every whim while his people live in abject misery?

Are you naive enough not to know that you were shown exactly what Saddam wanted you to see? Did he show you any of the torture chambers where he tortures little children to obtain confessions from their parents? Did he show you the underground tunnels where he stores his chemical and biological weapons? Did he show you any of the women who have been raped and horribly abused by his maniac son?

Don't you know that even if we lifted the embargo that the major part of the aid would never get to the people, that it would be taken away by Saddam and his henchmen?

What is it about Hollywood that so blinds you people to the evil in the world? Why do you insist that the United States is such a terrible nation?

The people of Iraq will only get the things they need when Saddam is six feet under the sand. He is the problem, he is the cause of the misery the Iraqi people are going through.

I did not even hear the words "Saddam Hussein" come out of your mouth—how can you be so blind? The Iraqi people's problems didn't start with the American embargo or even the first Gulf War. They started when Saddam came to power.

Iraq could be a rich and prosperous country if its leader didn't spend all its resources on military hardware and armies.

What about the billions of dollars he gets from France and Germany and the other countries he has oil deals with? Do you see him spending any of that money on food and medicine for his starving citizens?

How dare you blame Iraq's problems on the U.S.A. and have the nerve to come back to this country? You should have stayed and used some of the millions of dollars you've made in this evil nation to help the Iraqi citizens.

One thing about it, Mr. Penn, you will be remembered for a whole lot more than your acting. There will be hundreds of thousands of men and women who proudly wear the uniform of the United States of America who will remember you for a long time. They will remember that you went to an enemy country and gave aid and comfort not only to an enemy, but also to one of the most evil people on the face of the earth.

They will remember your words, criticizing the country they love enough to die for.

I wouldn't be going to any Veterans of Foreign War meetings if I were you, Mr. Penn.

By the way, do you remember Jane Fonda?

AN OPEN LETTER TO THE HOLLYWOOD BUNCH

OK, let's just say for a moment you bunch of pampered, overpaid, unrealistic children had your way and the U.S.A. didn't go into Iraq. Let's say that you really get your way and we destroy all our nuclear weapons and stick daisies in our gun barrels and sit around with some white wine and cheese and pat ourselves on the back, so proud of what we've done for world peace.

Let's say that we cut the military budget to just enough to keep the National Guard on hand to help out with floods and fires.

Let's say that we close down our military bases all over the world and bring the troops home, increase our foreign aid, and drop all the trade sanctions against everybody.

I suppose that in your fantasy world this would create a utopian world where everybody would live in peace. After all, the great monster, the United States of America, the cause of all the world's trouble, would have disbanded its horrible military and certainly all the other countries of the world would follow suit.

After all, they only arm themselves to defend their countries from the mean old U.S.A.

Why, you bunch of pitiful, hypocritical, idiotic, spoiled mugwumps. Get your heads out of the sand and smell the Twin Towers burning.

Do you think that a trip to Iraq by Sean Penn did anything but encourage a wanton murderer to think that the people of the U.S.A. didn't have the nerve or the guts to fight him?

Barbra Streisand's fanatical and hateful rantings about George Bush make about as much sense as Michael Jackson hanging a baby over a railing.

You people need to get out of Hollywood once in a while and get out into the real world. You'd be surprised at the hostility you would find out here.

Stop in at a truck stop and tell an overworked, long-distance truck driver that you don't think Saddam Hussein is doing anything wrong.

Tell a farmer with a couple of sons in the military that you think the United States has no right to defend itself.

Go down to Baxley, Georgia, and hold an antiwar rally and see what the folks down there think about you.

You people are some of the most disgusting examples of a waste of protoplasm I've ever had the displeasure to hear about.

Sean Penn, you're a traitor to the United States of America. You gave aid and comfort to the enemy. How many American lives will your little "fact-finding trip" to Iraq cost? You encouraged Saddam to think that we didn't have the stomach for war.

You people protect one of the most evil men on the face of this earth and won't lift a finger to save the life of an unborn baby. Freedom of choice, you say?

Well, I'm going to exercise some freedom of choice of my own. If I see any of your names on a marquee, I'm going to boycott the movie. I will completely stop going to movies if I have to. In most cases it certainly wouldn't be much of a loss.

You scoff at our military whose boots you're not even worthy to shine. They go to battle and risk their lives so ingrates like you can live in luxury.

The day of reckoning is coming when you will be faced with the undeniable truth that the war against Saddam Hussein is the war on terrorism.

America is in imminent danger. You're either for her or against her. There is no middle ground.

I think we all know where you stand.

TO OUR TROOPS

I know that a lot of you in the military have computers with you where you are serving because I get so much e-mail from you, and I thank you for it.

I wanted to tell you that the people of the U.S.A. are greatly in your debt.

You are on a noble mission and I know that you see things in the media from time to time that make you wonder just how solid your support in our nation is.

Well, let me tell you something, I travel this nation from coast to coast and border to border regularly. This year I will probably play for around a million people. I talk to an awful lot of them in the course of a year, and I tell you honestly that support for our armed services in this country is strong and pervasive.

Well, you may ask, how about the people who are demonstrating against us in the streets of American cities?

If you could go to those demonstrations and walk among the people there you would be surprised to know that, especially in the large cities, there are people there who represent the Communist Party, the anti–International Monetary Fund bunch, radical women's groups, and just anybody else on the fringe of American politics with an ax to grind.

Also this is actually more of a political protest than antiwar protest. This is actually for the most part a protest against your commander in chief. They just don't like anything about George Bush and just can't accept the fact that Al Gore didn't win the election.

If you notice the signs they carry none of them mention Saddam or that they support the military but don't like the war. No, they're about what an idiot President Bush is and compare him to people like Adolf Hitler.

Now that's about the most asinine thing I've ever heard. Think about this: did they get out in the street and demonstrate against Bill Clinton when he started shooting off cruise missiles?

Did they criticize Clinton for the military actions he started?

The mission you are on is not only necessary, it is urgent.

The anti-war demonstrators will tell you that they're worried about collateral damage, but I guarantee you that when this is over the world will have to admit that Saddam Hussein has killed a hundred times more of his people intentionally than your forces ever will unintentionally.

You see, that's what I can't understand about these people.

Does it matter to them that five thousand children a month starve to death in Iraq? Or that Saddam has people shredded in plastic shredders like a piece of thrown away paper, or that he has little children tortured by his goons, or that he has men's wives raped in their presence, or that he has ruined the economy of a country which could be modern and prosperous, or that he and his chosen few live in royal luxury while the people of Iraq starve?

They say, "Well, it hasn't been proven to me that he has weapons of mass destruction."

Well, just hang on, y'all. The day is fast approaching when you will see the evidence that Saddam does have weapons of mass destruction, and I just hope that you'll have the decency to thank the men and women in uniform who kept them from being used on you.

Thank you, troops. You do America proud.

NORTH KOREA

To say that Kim Jong Il, the dictator of North Korea, is a depraved evil man is like calling the Pacific Ocean a mud puddle.

He lives like King Midas while the people of North Korea starve and are deprived of the most basic of life's necessities. He has kept his nation in the dark about what's going on in the rest of the world. They only know what he will allow to be distributed by his state controlled media.

North Korea has not entered into the twentieth century, much less the twenty-first century.

If you were to look at a nighttime satellite shot of that part of the world you would see light in all the surrounding countries, while North Korea looks like a black hole because of the absence of electricity.

The deprived citizens of North Korea have cut down the majority of the trees for heat and cooking, causing erosion of the topsoil they so desperately need for their crops.

The degree of destitution in this pitiful nation is hard to grasp by us well-fed Westerners, who think that poverty is not owning a television set.

Mothers in Korea literally poison newborn babies to keep them from going through the horrible deprivation.

I have been to Korea three times and have talked with some of the military personnel who stand watch at the 38th Parallel, who passed along some of the things they had heard about Jong Il. He is a depraved monster who kidnaps women and keeps them as slaves for sex parties.

Now that's hard to believe in 2003; it sounds like something that would have happened back in medieval times when kings were absolute monarchs.

The people of North Korea need to be liberated. If the United Nations was anything besides a toothless debating society it would come down on North Korea with both feet.

While his people starve, Jong Il spends the meager resources of his country proliferating a nuclear program, and to think about a madman like him having nuclear weapons at his disposal is a horrifying thought.

And just who do you think he'd use these weapons against? I can only speculate. Certainly not against China or Russia.

My opinion is that Jong Il wants nuclear weapons for two reasons, to sell to terrorist nations for hard currency and to blackmail the rest of the world.

The Republic of Korea, or South Korea, has a standing army with some of the toughest soldiers you'll find anywhere.

The United States has 37,000 crack troops in South Korea with all the latest military hardware and technology. And they are prepared to rain destruction down on North Korea at any time that it should be required.

But of course nobody wants it to come to that, and I pray that it doesn't.

Now for all you people who are preaching containment for Saddam Hussein, learn a lesson from this: Containment just doesn't work. North Korea has been bottled up for fifty years and is still one of the most dangerous and volatile countries on earth.

Evil cannot be contained; evil is evil and is going to either flourish or be stamped out. Jong Il and Saddam Hussein need to be stamped out.

Nobody suffers worse under their cruelty than their own people.

What needs to be understood here by the world community is that it is not just the United States which is in danger, it is every free-thinking, democratic nation on earth.

If this country ever needed to be united it is now, and I call on everybody in Washington to put your politics aside and let's show the world a united front.

I don't call on you Hollywood people to do anything because nobody pays any attention to you anyway; you're just preaching to each other.

BRINGING IT ALL BACK HOME

It seems every which way we turn these days we're catching it from somebody. Even our neighbors to the north in Canada have been pretty vocal in their criticism of our policies, with one of their diplomats calling our president a not-so-nice name.

Germany, France, and Belgium have refused to back an invasion of Iraq.

It seems that America is not wanted in many parts of the world, and I have a proposal.

Let's rescind the NAFTA Treaty. We're the short end of the stick there anyway. What do we need with NAFTA anyway?

Let's boycott Perrier water and French wine and discourage Americans from spending their hard-earned dollars vacationing in a country which would be speaking German if not for the U.S. military.

Let's close down all our military bases in Germany and relocate them in the United States. The billions of dollars in payroll would boost the economy and also the morale of our troops serving at home instead of a foreign country.

Let's uncap our oil wells in the western states and put the alternative fuel program on the fast track. There again our economy would flourish, and if I'm going to pay two dollars a gallon for gas I want it to come out of the ground in America.

Let's turn all our military might to eradicating terrorism instead of protecting countries that don't appreciate it. Maybe even countries that helped Saddam Hussein develop his chemical weapons program.

Let's close our borders down tight to all but legal immigrants and deport those illegals who are already here. That would go a long way in doing away with terrorists.

Let's declare a real war on drugs and crime. With the money we save by not having to have a standing army in Germany we could have plenty of manpower and all the technical bells and whistles.

Let's raise the pay for our military and let the men and women who defend us make a living wage.

Let's find out who our friends really are and protect them from their enemies—in fact their enemies should be our enemies and vice versa. No more of this French and German back stabbing.

Let's stop investing, manufacturing, or trading with these nations. Believe me, it won't be long before they'll feel the economic sting.

Let's just bring everybody home and solve our own problems and let those who are not our allies solve their own. Let's see how soon they start to squeal when the Osama bin Ladens of the world find out that the price for attacking the U.S.A. is way too high and start blowing up buildings and people in their countries.

Then when they go to the United Nations and want to attack the monsters we can sit back and say no, what we need is a diplomatic solution. Give the inspectors a few more months while the suicide bombers continue to tear you apart. You've just not proved the necessity of bombing to our satisfaction. And then let's build a missile defense system for us and our allies and sit back and thumb our nose at the world.

If we would seriously consider even part of these policies, you would see an immediate change in the attitudes of the rest of the world.

Let's do it.

AN OPEN LETTER TO A LAWYER WHOSE NAME I FORGET, BUT WHOSE STUPIDITY I NEVER WILL

The other night I was watching television when another flower-mouthed bleeding heart, liver, and lungs kind of guy came on decrying the treatment of the al Qaeda prisoners in Cuba and spouting off about how they should be brought to the United States and given a jury trial and about how their constitutional rights were being trampled on and so on. It was all I could do to keep from throwing up.

In the first place, you pompous ass, these people have no constitutional rights. You should get a copy of the Constitution of the United States and read it. In the opening it clearly states that "We the people of the United States" are who the Constitution is talking about, not a bunch of murdering foreign slobs like the scum they're holding in Guantanamo Bay.

Then he was raving about the Geneva conference on the treatment of prisoners of war. These people are common criminals, not prisoners of war; they have no rights in this country or any other, for that matter. They are enemies of every civilized country on the face of this earth.

They should be tried by a military tribunal. They deserve quick and decisive justice and if they all end up in front of a firing squad that's the breaks of the game they're playing in.

In taking up for these scumballs you insult every person who has a friend or relative who was wantonly murdered on 9-11 by the very people you are so concerned with defending. And when the commentator confronted you with this truth you responded by saying, "I will not play on the emotionalism of the war." Well let me tell you something, you overeducated numbskull, you'd darn well better start playing on the emotionalism of the war before you wake up one morning breathing poison gas.

Who do you think these people are? A bunch of wayward Boy Scouts who are in danger of losing their merit badges?

Of course you and your ilk would like to get them over here and put on a show trial so you and all the rest of your lawyer buddies could get your faces on television and fatten your pocketbooks.

People like you literally make me sick. I seriously doubt if you'd lift your manicured little finger to save the life of an innocent unborn child who is about to suffer a painful death at the hands of an abortionist. Yet you exhibit your rank stupidity by defending a gang of scraps who would like nothing better than to cut your throat.

You and all like you weaken the resolve of this great nation. You rant and rave about injustice when you wouldn't know injustice if it bit you on your padded posterior. How about the injustice of the murder of thousands of innocent people who did nothing more than go to work one morning? How about the injustice of the children of firemen and policemen whose mothers and daddies will never again sit down at the dinner table with them? How about the injustice of women who were treated no better than cattle by these people? How about the injustice of our airlines being pirated and crashed into our national icons?

You're a national disgrace, sir, and I say to heck with you and the ten-speed bicycle you rode in on.

DEMONSTRATIONS

I don't question anyone's right to demonstrate for or against anything they want to. It is a right which we enjoy by living in the United States of America. You have a right to demonstrate, I have a right to say how I feel about it.

Let's just say, for the sake of argument, that you live in San Francisco and you went to Washington for an anti-war protest rally, and while you were gone someone set off a suitcase-sized nuclear device in the tenderloin and killed 500,000 people. And what if the weapon were traced to Saddam Hussein's arsenal in Iraq?

The first thing you would say is, "Why didn't the government do something to stop this? Why didn't they know about this and preempt it?"

Well, my fellow American, your government does know about it and they are trying to do something about it. I can't understand how anyone can even entertain the idea that Saddam does not have nuclear and biological weapons and is not developing a delivery system.

The inspectors are not going to find a smoking gun. Hussein is evil but he's not an idiot, he can play cat and mouse with a handful of inspectors for years.

The 9-11 tragedy was caused by trusting the wrong people and being negligent. Bill Clinton had the opportunity to have

Osama bin Laden in U.S. custody not once but three times. He didn't do it, and look what happened.

Why should we do the same thing with Saddam? It's idiocy. Of course war is horrible, of course there are going to be civilian casualties, and of course there are going to be body bags. But that's nothing compared to the civilian casualties and body bags we will suffer down the road if Saddam is left in power.

The people of Iraq suffer needlessly under this cruel tyrant. His son is a sadist who rapes whomever he wants to for sport. How would you like for somebody to pick your daughter up off the street, viciously rape her, maybe even kill her, and there would be absolutely nothing you could do about it?

How would you like to watch your children do without the essentials of life just because a maniacal dictator wants to hold on to power?

If Saddam had the military might that we have, do you think he would attack us with no regard for the innocent women and children he would murder? Of course he would, and the longer we wait the closer he will come to being able to hold the world hostage with a nuclear or biological threat.

Look at what's happening in Korea: Kim Jong Il is another loose cannon, volatile and dangerous. His father and he have starved and deprived the North Korean people for decades forcing them to live in poverty we can only imagine. While South Korea prospers, North Korea starves. And why? Just because a bunch of thugs are possessed with power?

They have cut down most of their trees to use for fuel, the land is eroding, the people are hungry, and what is Kim Jong Il's reaction? To develop nuclear weapons? These despots care nothing for their country and its people; all they care about is raw power.

Saddam is not a man of peace, he's slaughtered his own people, he's gone to war with Iran and invaded Kuwait and left behind him the worst man-made ecological disaster in history when he set fire to the Kuwaiti oil fields.

So before you get on another bus and head for that antiwar protest rally, think about whom you are trying to attack. I know you don't think about it in those terms, but if you'll consider the facts, and be honest with yourself, you'll come to that conclusion.

GROUND ZERO

I just returned from Ground Zero in New York City where some 2,800 people lost their lives on September 11, 2001. I would like to thank the Port Authority Police for the guided tour and the courtesy they showed us while we were there. I don't think that everybody realizes that they lost thirty-seven of their brothers in the Trade Tower explosion, the most officers ever lost in a single incident.

When you think about those majestic towers which dominated the skyline of lower Manhattan for so many years being reduced to a gigantic hole in the ground and think about the thousands of innocent people who came to work that morning without an inkling of what was about to happen, it has to touch your heart.

You can see Ground Zero on television but you can't feel it. You can't feel the resolve of the police and fire departments or the red-blooded Americanism of the on-site construction workers.

You don't hear about the guys who operated the giant machines and drove them out onto piles of burning rubble while fire hoses sprayed water around them as they dug into the mess. You don't see the poster with the picture of the thirty-seven Port Authority officers who died heroes' deaths there. You can't feel the anger that you experience as you stand there trying to imagine what it must have been like that Tuesday morning.

It's hard to believe that an atrocity of this magnitude has been carried out on American soil.

It makes you want to grab Osama bin Laden and the rest of his scumballs by the throat.

It makes you realize that no matter what it takes we have to do everything in our power to prevent this from happening again.

Our senators and congressmen have already started posturing to make political hay out of this war we're engaged in, and I think that it's a dangerous move. Any politician who tries to take advantage of this situation for purely political reasons is harming this country and should be voted out of office.

This is a time for unity, a time for putting aside political aspirations and partisan cat fights, sniping and whining, rhetoric and personal or party gains, and forget we're Democrats or Republicans, conservative or liberal, and come together and use a little common sense for the common good of this nation.

This country is crying out for justice for the thousands of innocent people killed in this country on September 11 and doesn't want to sit around and wait for a bunch of party hacks to sit around and debate the pros and cons of protecting this country from another attack.

Besides, what's the mystery about that? We know who the bad guys are. Let's just go get 'em. Let's stop pretending that Saudi Arabia is our friend when we know it's not. Let's get on with the job of doing away with Saddam Hussein. Let's put aside the political correctness and give our intelligence agencies the laws and the tools they need to track down terrorists in America. Let's deport the illegal immigrants.

We need to stop our dependency on foreign oil by developing our reserves in Alaska and other areas. It can be done without risk to the environment regardless of what the radical environmentalists try to shove down our throats.

I'm for whatever it takes to win this war and protect this nation. No more holes in the ground where Americans lost their lives. No more 9-11s.

THE BIG KID

It seems to me that there are some people in this country who are ashamed that America is the last and only superpower on earth. They act as if they are ashamed of what America has become, and every time we are forced to flex our muscle they come out of the woodwork to preach doom and gloom for the future of our nation.

They mistakenly touted the strength of the Republican Guard in the Gulf War as if they were an unbeatable military force that we would meet our match in.

Well, we all know what happened. We all saw the television pictures of half-starved Iraqi military forces surrendering on their knees to our troops.

One pitiful batch of Iraqis even surrendered to an Italian television crew.

Afghanistan will be another Vietnam, they said. Look at what happened to the Russians. There was a vast difference in what Russia was trying to do in Afghanistan and what we were doing there. Russia went there to conquer and occupy Afghanistan. We went there to liberate it.

Sometimes it seems that with the exception of a handful of nations, the world at large takes a poke at us every chance it gets. What other motive could France have in its recent behavior in the United Nations than to bring the U.S.A. down a notch or two?

They could just as easily have said that they opposed the war with Iraq and abstained from voting on the Security Council. They didn't have to threaten a veto and fly their diplomats around the world in an attempt to erode our support.

Mark my words. When the terrorist attacks begin in Paris, and they will, the French will come around screaming like a stuck pig begging for our help. And you know what? We will help them. Why? Because we're the big kid on the block. We're the only hope of free nations.

When Chrissy Hynde made her asinine statement about hoping that the Iraqis defeated us in the war, she should have thought about what would happen to her own country if her wish had come true. What would happen to England without the U.S.A.? Who would help them? The French? The French are afraid of their own shadow. The only war they ever won was the French Revolution, and that's just because they were fighting each other.

And I think that their other Western European allies have shown their true colors.

Many brave men and women have died so that America could be a free and sovereign nation, so that we could stand on our own and protect our own interests. Not so that we could kowtow to the impotence of the United Nations or allow a despot like Saddam Hussein to rape, torture, and abuse a whole population of helpless citizens.

America is the big kid on the block, and I for one am proud of it.

This is a dangerous world we live in, and there are a lot of people in it who would like nothing better than to reduce the U.S.A. to a pile of rubble.

Saddam Hussein is one of them, and our dedicated troops who fight in Iraq are serving a dual purpose. To free the people of Iraq and free Planet Earth of terrorism.

Fight on, brave ones, we're right behind you.

Pray for our troops.

AN OPEN LETTER TO THE MEDIA

I thank God for freedom of the press, unhampered by government control. It is a blessing which is nonexistent in a lot of countries.

But with freedom comes responsibility, and in the case of the media this should constitute fairness, telling both sides of the story. Opinion- and agenda-driven journalism should be relegated to the editorial page.

The American people need to know the truth, the whole truth, which means reporting things that go outside the boundaries of personal politics. Even if it makes the other side look good once in a while.

I'm glad to see Fox News come on line; at least they usually give both sides of the story. They are often accused of being a conservative network but the truth of the matter is that this nation has not heard TV coverage which has not been tilted to the left in so long that when they do get fair and balanced coverage to some liberals it seems conservative.

For instance, the other night one of their correspondents interviewed some of the antiwar protesters asking them what the alternative to going to war with Iraq would be. The standard answer was, "I don't know."

So here are a bunch of young people out in the street demonstrating against a war and they don't even know why. Does this make any sense? And why didn't Peter Jennings and company talk to some of these people?

And I don't mean that Fox is perfect but they sure report more of the news than the other channels do.

And why don't the media tell the truth about abortion, that it is profit driven, and why can't they show a partial birth abortion? Too gruesome, you say? Well just how gruesome is it for the baby who is being cruelly murdered?

And why do they try to pillory a man like Billy Graham who has devoted every hour of his adult life to good works, by quoting an old statement which was taken out of context concerning Jews? Billy Graham loves the Jews and Israel, the media know that, but they just don't care. I think that's not telling the whole story, but is irresponsible journalism.

And what about coverage of the Islamic prisoners in Guantanamo Bay? Why don't they tell the military's side of that story?

And why do they follow Jesse Jackson and Al Sharpton around like loyal puppy dogs ignoring Jackson's shady financial dealings and Sharpton's propensity for causing violence?

And why do they love to tell us bad news about the economy when there's also good things happening?

I know the reason why. The network news and many of the large newspapers in this country have a liberal political agenda and they know that if the news is presented fairly that you'll be less likely to swallow their line and go along with their thinking.

The front page of a newspaper should not look like the editorial page.

Think about it, do you ever wonder why the *Washington Post* and the *New York Times* seldom have anything good to say about President Bush? Doesn't he ever do anything that deserves praise?

And do you ever wonder why they never say anything bad about Hillary Clinton? Doesn't she do something once in a while that deserves criticism?

Think about the kind of America these people are pushing for and be extremely careful how much of their coverage you believe. Is it the truth, the whole truth, and nothing but the truth?

MEMORIAL DAY

On Sunday, Memorial Day weekend, alone in a hotel room in Cleveland, Ohio, I saw the movie *Saving Private Ryan*. As I watched the vivid reenactment of brave men fighting and dying on the beaches of Normandy my mind hearkened back to a sunny morning in Valdosta, Georgia, when my mother woke me up early and we went to our church to pray for the sons and fathers of America who were storming the dug-in German placements in the bloody battle that came to be known as D-Day.

I had never seen the church so full. It was packed as concerned parents, wives, and children came together to plead for Almighty God's protection on our precious loved ones who were in harm's way so far away from us.

Scene after scene of incredible carnage brought home the old adage that war is indeed hell.

As I watched the bloodshed and remembered the day, I wept openly and unashamed.

I wept for the brave men who lost their lives defending our country. I wept for the parents who received the dreaded letter from the War Department. I wept for the children who never really got to know their fathers, and I wept for our nation and what it has become.

I think that we have gotten to the point that we take our military for granted.

We tend to think of our armed forces as some monolithic, faceless entity which pops up at the trouble spots and flash points of the world. Some impersonal band of uniforms which can be put in harm's way at the whim of an inept and corrupt president or sent halfway around the world to serve under the impotent blue banner of the United Nations.

Well, folks, these are our sons and daughters, the very cream of American youth, and I think it's high time that they started receiving the respect they deserve.

We need to restore the appropriations that have been systematically taken away and diverted to other pet projects that have absolutely nothing to do with the defense of this nation.

The reenlistment ratios have steadily fallen through the years until the levels have reached alarming proportions with undermanned aircraft carriers and not enough pilots to fly our high tech jets.

Young men and women who once made a career out of the military are going into the private sector in droves. What has happened?

Well, I have my own ideas about what has happened and I'm sure that you do too. Somehow we have to revitalize our military; we have to restore the pride and devotion that once motivated the young men of this nation to storm the beaches of Normandy.

VETERANS

The United States of America has always honored the people who fought for our freedoms on foreign soil. The ones who came home were revered and decorated and welcomed back with exuberant celebrations and patriotic articles in the newspapers, feting their heroism and acts of bravery.

And the ones who had given their all to preserve our way of life were remembered in memorial services and spoken about in reverent and hushed tones. This is as it should have been. When someone fights a war for their country they deserve undying gratitude and admiration from the ones who reap the benefit of their service. That's why I become incensed when I think about how our fighting men and women were treated when they returned from Vietnam.

When I think about brave men and women being spit on by dirty, stoned-out, jobless, pseudo-intellectual hippies whose only contribution to this nation had been to burn their draft cards, it makes my collar get about two sizes too small.

Not that I was in favor of the war. It became evident very early in the game that our politicians were not going to let us win that war.

What had started out as a noble effort to contain Communism became a futile exercise of "peace with honor" and "I don't want to be the first president to lose a war," while the cream of

American youth was being sacrificed to the god of political expedience in the jungles of Southeast Asia.

We could have won that war, if it would have been fought on the battlefield instead of the halls of Congress and the Oval Office.

You don't send people to war with one hand tied behind their backs: "Now you can't shoot at them unless they shoot at you first." Baloney; we're talking about war, not a game of ring around the roses.

In my book, when you go to war you shoot at the enemy every time you see him and you keep on shooting until he either surrenders or doesn't exist anymore. You throw everything you've got at him every hour of every day until you grind him into the dust. Bomb him; shoot him; overrun his positions; cut his supply lines, and do it consistently until you pound him into submission.

And then, after he is thoroughly beaten and you can deal from a position of absolute authority, sit down at the peace table with him, work out something sensible, and get our troops the heck out of there.

If we're not willing to go all out to define and attain victory, we should never, ever get into another war.

It took a chronic attack of the dumbass for somebody to blame the war in Vietnam on the people who fought it. Put the blame where it belongs and I think anybody with enough gray matter to cover a pinhead knows who that is: the politicians.

I've heard the flower child pipedream adage of "What if they gave a war and nobody came?"

To which I would add, "What if the United States of America was being attacked and everybody burned their draft cards and went to Canada?"

Now you mavens of political correctness, don't even bother e-mailing me to tell me what a fascist you think I am. I am not in favor of war or any other kind of bloodshed. I'm simply stating my belief that if we ever have to go to war again, let's go in with both barrels blazing and get it over with.

And a word to all you Vietnam vets: Just please know that there's a fat boy in Tennessee who holds every one of you in the utmost esteem and wishes to thank you for serving your country when the call came. May God bless each and every one of you and may God continue to bless our beloved United States of America.

SCHOOL SHOOTINGS

We all need to face this unholy phenomenon which is happening in our schools. It can happen anywhere in this nation. It is not restricted by size, academic standards nor neighborhoods.

What really brought it home to me was when a thirteen-year-old boy made a kill list and one of my friend's daughter's name was on it.

This was in a Christian school in a small community, something I never thought I'd see happen. Thank God he was discovered in the planning stages and no actual shooting occurred.

We have got to face this horrible problem head on. We can no longer think that it just happens to other people in other towns. It's an epidemic, a scourge, a nationwide plague with dire and sinister implications.

It's too late to nip it in the bud, but at least we can start doing something serious about it now.

What do we do? I certainly don't have all the answers, but I do believe I have some.

Our children are too impressionable and important to be subjected to the standards of political correctness. Some things are right and some things are wrong and no matter how diametrically the truth goes against today's social mores, children should be told the truth.

Some music is bad, some television programs are bad, some movies are bad, some behavior is unacceptable, and when you do something wrong there are consequences to pay.

There is absolutely no need to wait for the government to do anything. The things they do are for show and have to be done with the approval of the *Washington Post*.

We can't expect the entertainment industry to do anything because they're only motivated by profit, and just don't care.

It has to start at home at a very early age, and the most important part of the process is love. Do you hug your children? Do you ever take time to sit down and talk to them? Do you have any idea what they're doing when they're not around you? Are you willing to do them the favor of punishing them when they do something they know they shouldn't?

Are you letting a television set raise your child?

Do you not see the harm in letting them watch things you know are way off center? Don't you think that it will have an impression on them?

Well, let me tell you something, younger and younger children are practicing oral sex these days, children who didn't even know the meaning of the term until a certain scumbag president made it a household word.

And I can hear it now: if we could just not allow the public access to guns. Baloney, we can't even keep the public from having access to crack cocaine and it's already against the law and probably kills more people every year than guns do.

It's a sad thing to say, but children who take guns to school should be very severely punished and I'm not talking about a slap on the wrist.

The problem is way past being serious and we have got to face it and act to eradicate it, even if it means taking drastic steps. Steps that are distasteful but necessary.

GUN COMPANIES

Among the insanely ridiculous things that are happening in these asinine politically correct times is something which will set a dangerous and disastrous precedent in the United States of America.

And that is the suing of gun manufacturers by cities and other entities.

In the first place, the people who cause the trouble with the guns are not supposed to have them anyway and are going to obtain them through illegal sources no matter how many lawsuits and new laws are brought against the legal-weary legitimate businesses in this country.

The same people who want to bring lawsuits, the lawyers are the same people who keep these dangerous criminals on the streets to start with. On the one hand, they find a technicality to keep a killer out of prison and, on the other, want to reap a harvest of billions by suing the gun companies.

And I'll bet you a vintage Les Paul against a pack of chewing gum that they're the only ones who will reap any benefit from it. I hate cigarettes, I am totally convinced that they are killers and I wish that there would never be another one lit, but I don't hold the tobacco companies responsible for somebody killing themselves with them.

That's the responsibility of the individual. Nobody holds a gun, no pun intended, on them and makes them light up a cancer stick. It's their own choice.

I would love to see the same amount of energy expended in eradicating illegal drugs.

We're more concerned about nicotine than narcotics. I've never heard of someone sticking up a liquor store so he could buy a pack of Marlboros.

The same people who cry the loudest about the foul dastardly tobacco companies and firearms manufacturers are the same people who tell us that we need drug education to stop kids from using them.

Well, how about tobacco education?

I haven't seen one person who has quit smoking because some scumbag lawyer has made another ten million dollars off the tobacco companies.

And now we want to put Smith and Wesson out of business because the bad boys have guns.

It's a strange thing to me that all these ruptured hearts remain silent when the Chinese bring in a shipment of assault rifles to sell to the street gangs in Los Angeles.

Scenario: Jealous lover runs over mate with sports utility vehicle. Lawyers sue all manufacturers of SUVs and are looking into the possibility of suing automakers.

Sounds silly doesn't it? But no sillier than suing gun manufacturers did a few years ago.

Once this Pandora is out of the box, there'll be no stopping it. Can't you just see somebody suing the stock exchange for losing money?

Don't laugh, these are the same people who protect us from such dangerous things as peanuts on airlines and nativity scenes in public places, and nearly faint at a copy of the Ten Commandments hanging on a judge's wall.

These are the same people who wink at the moral shortcomings of the most powerful man in the world and go ballistic when a minister of the Gospel shows his human side.

They had a lot of trouble with guns in the Old West. To get the guns out of society, they got the bad guys out of society.

PARTIAL BIRTH ABORTION

Anybody who thinks that partial birth abortion is not murder plain and simple is a blind ignorant idiot who refuses to acknowledge the truth when it is right there before him.

First-hand accounts bring home the fact that these babies are living human beings who are coldly and brutally butchered by some sleazy doctor whose greed overcomes his good sense.

The Holocaust pales in comparison when it comes to the loss of human life, and this disgraceful state of affairs is no less horrible than what happened in Nazi Germany.

The truth is that the majority of the people in this country are opposed to partial birth abortion. A bill cleared Congress abolishing it only to be vetoed by Bill Clinton, who in theory now has the blood of millions of innocents on his grubby hands.

But never mind, his case is on the docket in the court of eternal justice where the souls of unborn millions will stand in witness against his callous act of infanticide.

The people who condone this homicide are almost as guilty as the heartless doctors who perform it.

And the media will not be held blameless. They inundate us with buzz phrases like "pro-choice" and "a woman's right to choose," which so dehumanize the act of abortion that it is no longer viewed as what it is, cold-blooded murder.

When a fetus is taken from a mother's womb and a sharp instrument is plunged into its brain, how can it be described in any other way than the taking of innocent life? A baby is no less alive at that time than it is when it is three years old.

What is odd is that some of the people who are rabid defenders of animal rights favor partial birth abortion. The same people who are horrified at the inhuman killing of baby seals will not lift a finger or raise a whisper to save human life.

Of all the people who have lived on this earth since Adam and Eve I truly believe that the people of the United States of America are among the most blessed.

God has given us a beautiful land rich in fertile soil and natural resources. He has made us victorious in war and a world leader in technology and science. We live in a land of opportunity and freedom and, regardless of what the politically correct, humanist crowd says, it's all because of the blessings of Almighty God.

He has been patient with us, He has stood by and watched prayer taken from public schools, He has seen the ACLU try to take His name off every public place where it appears, He has seen our slow slide into decadence, and yet He has been merciful.

But how much more is God going to allow? This nation flies in His holy face by exalting those who deny His very existence. His Son's name is used as a swear word, mocked and joked about openly. His commandments are ignored and the liberal clergy say that we should interpret God's word to fit our modern-day lifestyles. And now we have slaughtered millions and millions of innocent babies, some by actually stabbing them to death.

God's word says that He knew us in our mother's womb and knitted the pieces together, so we know by the authority of our Creator that a fetus is a living being.

Now I know that there are people who don't believe in God and His teachings and His laws. To those people I would say that you can believe it now or you can believe it later, but in the endless reaches in eternity you will know beyond a shadow of a doubt that God does exist and that He hates abortion, partial birth or otherwise.

CHILD ABUSE

I hate violent crime. If you've read this column at all, you probably know how I feel about rape and murder and how I detest stealing and violence.

But of all the crimes that disgust me, the one which absolutely incenses me is child abuse.

I have heard all the half-baked excuses made by defense lawyers about environment, mental disorder, and all the other claptrap reasons they use to try to keep these sleazeballs from facing the music.

I could believe that extenuating circumstances may have some bearing on a lot of crimes, but not when it comes to child abuse.

I cannot find a way to believe that anybody could be so depraved or crazy that they don't know that it's wrong to hurt a child. Hurting someone innocent and defenseless is just about the lowest down thing anybody can do. Let's call it what it is, not environment or mental disorder but old-fashioned evil straight from the pit of hell itself.

Anybody who finds something erotic about a three-year-old girl or boy is not motivated by something from their past but by Satan himself.

It seems that as time goes by there's more and more child abuse and it's a sickening fact that we seem to do less and less about it. And when I say doing something about it I'm not talking about another study group or some overeducated fool claiming that this or that monster has an excuse for their despicable behavior.

No, I'm talking about taking these scumbags off the street. While so many judges are so concerned about the rights of criminals. Our children are suffering unspeakable horrors at the hands of depraved maniacs who stalk the innocent with abandon. Can you tell me how a person who has raped, tortured, dismembered, and murdered a child has the right to live much less walk the streets among helpless children again?

And yet our judicial system continues to turn them back out on the street time after time.

If I had my way I would take a branding iron and brand a big C.A. right in the middle of the forehead of everyone who seriously abuses a child. At least that way we'd know who they are.

Cruel, you say? What about what the pervert does to the child—is that not cruel?

No, these people are a special breed of degenerate, even hated by the rest of the criminal community.

Why do judges keep putting children back in homes where they are abused again and again? Why is the death penalty seldom applied when someone kills a child, and why do we put up with this menace?

Wake up, America. Let's rid ourselves of these slinking, shadowy animals who ruin lives and families and harm one of God's most precious possessions.

Children can't protect themselves, they trust us to do it. Don't you think it's time we earned that trust by insisting that child abusers be dealt with swiftly, decisively and harshly?

HOW LOW CAN YOU GO?

I always knew that the ACLU was anti-American, anti-God, and anti–just about everything else that I hold dear and sacred. I've never had much use for them or the left-wing agenda they promote. But I never thought that they would sink to the level that they have recently. This time they're sucking the scum off the bottom of the barrel.

NAMBLA (North American Man/Boy Love Association) is an outfit which advocates grown men having sex with under-aged boys. Their motto is "Eight is too late." I literally have a hard time writing about this bunch of slime balls because I get so enraged that I want to put my hands around somebody's neck and squeeze real hard.

Having sex with anyone underage, boy or girl, is totally illegal and what they do is openly promote crime.

Two of their members recently raped and murdered a little boy and the boy's father is suing this despicable outfit for contributing to the murder of his son. And guess who has volunteered to defend this garbage? The good old ACLU; that's who. Men and women who are supposedly bound to uphold the law are defending an organization whose reason for being is to break the law.

Oh, of course they claim that it's a First Amendment right of this bunch of perverted trash to say what they say. What this statement amounts to is what is dug up in the barnyards of America every day.

It simply doesn't hold water, and I can't even articulate the contempt in which I hold them for perverting a document as precious as the Constitution.

How can they honestly believe that the founding fathers who wrote the Constitution meant it for such a purpose? They would turn over in their collective graves if they were presented with such a travesty.

How could any decent man or woman stand in front of a jury and honestly say that these people have a right to advocate having sex with innocent children?

This is another by-product of homosexuality, and anyone who says that it is a natural lifestyle should go and stick their heads under some very cold water.

Homosexuality is not a normal thing and has produced some of the most brutal, gory murders in the history of this nation. Don't take my word for it. Ask any homicide officer in the country. Is this normal?

It ruins the lives of young people. I have a friend whose son was molested at a very early age and he has had serious mental problems ever since. Is this normal?

AIDS was introduced into America by gay sex, which opened Pandora's box, and I don't believe the lid will ever be found. Is this normal?

Before someone out there blows a gasket, let me say that I do not, I repeat, do not hate gay people. I would never even dream of being violent or even hostile to them. I am simply stating a fact: men having sex with young boys is a homosexual act.

I hope that people everywhere will think before they give any more money to the ACLU. It will be a cold day on the equator before they get a cent out of me. As for NAMBLA, something really needs to be done about this manure pile. Castration comes to mind.

But vengeance is mine, saith the Lord.

MOB RULE

The shameful thing that happened in Central Park the other day with thugs groping and tearing women's clothes off, and the near riot that took place in Los Angeles after the Lakers won the NBA title pretty much sums up the dilemma which our law enforcement officers find themselves in these days. Damned if they do and damned if they don't.

Had the mob been made up of Caucasians, they could have waded into the middle of it with nightsticks and mace and had the streets cleared in a matter of minutes. However, that was not the case: the thugs were mostly minorities so the police had to handle the situation with kid gloves lest Al Sharpton and his brother blowhards come forth and accuse them of racial profiling.

Every time someone says something like what I am getting ready to say, some loudmouthed hack comes out to call them a bigot.

Well, I am not a bigot, nor am I racially prejudiced, so I'll say what I dern well please and let the chips fall where they will. I know my heart.

A great disservice is being done to the minorities by the politicians of this country. They literally create the poverty that they claim to care so much about. They supply the resources which promote laziness and destroy the work ethic, creating generation after generation of welfare kids who don't even know who their fathers are.

They are raised by mothers who have found out that the more children they have the more money they get and a lot of that money ends up in the pockets of the local drug dealer.

They are raised in neighborhoods where violence is a way of life and the sound of gunshots is as commonplace as thunder.

For all the lofty talk our politicians make about education they send these kids to schools with unqualified teachers where the classroom is unruly and discipline is just a word.

Lacking parental nurturing, many of these kids find the companionship they so desperately need in street gangs which puts them at odds with the law.

Unfortunately, the rate of crime is much higher in minority neighborhoods, and it is an injustice to the hardworking decent folks to allow it to continue because some self-serving buffoon like Al Sharpton brings his bullhorn and proclaims racial prejudice at every serious attempt to enforce the law.

If he really wanted to do something for his people he would use his bullhorn and the media which follows him around like a puppy to denounce the drug dealers who prey on the people with much more devastating effect that the police department.

The men and women who enforce our laws are placed in an untenable position. Political correctness and the lack of responsible leadership in the minorities' communities have brought about a Mexican standoff. They can't win. If they do what needs doing they are accused of overreacting and if they stand by and do nothing they are accused of under-reacting.

In these days of violence and lawlessness it is tough enough being a police officer without being criticized for every move you make.

I wonder what's going to happen when the violence makes its way out to where Al Sharpton lives and he needs the police to protect his life and property.

REPARATIONS

One of the most ridiculous and racially divisive issues to come along in a very long time is the one about the government paying reparations to blacks because of slavery.

This is absolutely asinine. First of all, even if they were entitled to reparations, which they certainly are not, who would get the money? How would it be distributed? Could you just show up at a federal agency and if your skin was dark enough would they fork over the bucks? How about the people who have migrated to America since the Civil War, do they get a piece of the pie?

How can the present-day citizens of this country be held accountable for something which happened before their great-grandparents were born?

There's no question about it, slavery was an abomination and I don't know anybody who thinks it wasn't, but so were a lot of other things, and they are all best relegated to the history books and viewed as a lesson learned.

My family never owned slaves. Should I have to pay just because my skin is white? And since this money would be coming from the public coffers, how about the black citizens who would be taxed right along with the rest of us to pay for this pie-in-the-sky folly?

The self-righteous pundits I see on television say it's about justice, but it has nothing to do with justice since the very concept is totally unjust. No sir, this has to do with greed, money, power and furthering the agenda of a handful of radicals who like nothing better than driving a wedge between the races.

These people thrive off racial dissension, it's all that keeps them in power. As long as they can convince a percentage of the African American population in this nation that they are inferior and have to have help from the big government, they can make a place for themselves under the guise of furthering the cause.

Black Americans have come a long way in the last forty years and now some of these self-proclaimed leaders would lead them backwards. If they really wanted to do some good for their people they would encourage the young to finish school and develop a sense of self-worth and independence rather than giving them the same old line about whitey wanting to hold them down.

I'm white and I don't want to hold anyone down. I want to encourage all Americans to achieve their goals and make a better life for them and their families.

Black people are not inferior to anybody and that has been proven time after time in the twentieth century.

Why can't we put the past behind us and strive for the goal of a color-blind society, where black Americans, white Americans, Mexicans, Asians, Christians and Jews will just be known as simply Americans?

Slavery ended almost 150 years ago and everybody who ever owned a slave has been dead for years, and though it was the black Africans who sold their own people into slavery I haven't heard anything about suing them, which would be just as silly as suing the American government.

This is just a ploy to put off the inevitable fact that it's time for African Americans and all races, for that matter, to take their places in the higher echelons of business and politics.

Slavery is a blight on the history of America. It has already done its damage one time. Let's not resurrect this horrible thing to do more damage to racial relations.

AMERICANS

African Americans, Asian Americans, Native Americans, Cuban Americans: Is all of this necessary?

Are we not all Americans, and do these categorizations of our diverse cultural groups not encourage division and separation? Is not one of the basic premises of our democracy that "All men are created equal"?

I know what you're thinking, that I'm just a naive country boy who is either unable or unwilling to recognize the complexities of life in America today, the prejudice, the partiality, the downright evil ignorance which some people cling to so tenaciously.

Nothing could be farther from the truth. I was born and bred in the Heart of Dixie when Jim Crow was a reality, when black people were looked upon as being genetically inferior to Caucasians and were treated accordingly.

I never went to school with even one black child, I never sat in a restaurant, a movie theater, nor any other public facility with any black person.

Black people were relegated to the back of the bus, the balcony of the movie theaters, the other side of the restaurant, and the bathrooms and drinking fountains which were marked "colored." They went to supposedly "separate but equal" schools. Well, at least half of that was true, the separate part, but the equal part was about as far from the truth as you can get.

The truth was in most cases, they went to school in run-down, drafty old buildings and rode there on run-down old school buses. It was a struggle for a black kid to get an education. With rare exceptions the whole race was looked upon as slow, lazy and untrustworthy. People who had too many children and murdered the King's English, a knife-toting, whiskey-drinking, shiftless subculture who were content with their second class citizenship and blissfully happy with their lot. This inherited misconception was bad enough on our part, but what was even sadder is the fact that we were right!!!! We thought that things were supposed to be this way.

How did I find out different? I figured it out for myself. That's right; I looked around me and said in essence, "This ain't right." I am happy to say that early in my life I overcame racial prejudice on my own without any help from the ACLU, the United States Congress or any liberal think tank. I did it on my own many years ago.

In my eyes an American is an American is an American, skin color and racial genetics notwithstanding. When we refer to each other as African Americans and so forth, aren't we practicing a subtle form of mental segregation? Isn't it time that we dropped the adjective and just use the noun?

I feel that there are factions in this country who profit greatly from keeping the races off balance. Politicians seeking power blocs and activists on all sides of the racial issue seek to divide us for their own purposes.

Well, it's high time that we stopped this political correctness–foolishness and got down to where the rubber meets the road, and I'll start the ball rolling.

Whoever you are, whatever you are, I extend the hand of brotherhood to you. I pledge to treat you fairly and courteously, with respect and dignity befitting one of God's unique creations. I will not mistreat you nor label you in any way; to me you are an American, just an American.

Won't you join me, America?

ALIENS

The recent action by the Congress giving amnesty to illegal aliens really puts the icing on the cake for me. Blanket amnesty is never a good thing, as it rewards the guilty as well as the innocent.

Now I have absolutely nothing against any person who seeks entry into the U.S.A. to become a productive member of society. To work hard and raise a family that contributes to the American way of life.

But we all know that the element that sneaks across the border contains drug dealers and other undesirables who not only do nothing for society but try to tear it down. Why do we even have borders if we're going to allow anybody who can violate them to stay here without any penalty at all? It's also not fair to the millions who have come before and worked hard to get here and earned their citizenship the legal way.

I sometimes think that the politicians in Washington live in a different country from the rest of us. They create laws never considering the effect on nor the ramifications to the people who actually have to live under them. I think it should be required that every elected public official should have to keep office hours in the territory they were elected in and have conversations with the people who elected them to find out what's really on the minds of the everyday citizens of this nation and not just what they are told by the high-priced lobbyists who wine and dine them on a regular basis.

I believe that they should be required to spend three months out of every year listening to the opinions of the real people. I know one thing, if our elected officials who voted for this amnesty had spent time in my neck of the woods they would have gotten an earful. They should also be limited as to the amount of terms they can serve. They should serve eight years and then come home and work for a living just like the rest of us. Then we would have a fresh view of the issues, with someone fresh off the streets speaking their mind instead of some jaded old blowhard who considers political alliances and being reelected more important than what is good for the country.

We need politicians who will vote their consciences and to hell with the party line. We need politicians who will not stand by and let the reputation of a good man be slandered as in the recent case of Judge Pickering. We need politicians who will stand up and condemn a lying, cheating, self-serving traitor like Bill Clinton, regardless of what the rest of his party does. We need politicians who will tell us the truth instead of sugar-coating it to make themselves look good. We need patriots, not cowards, doers and not talkers, we need representatives, not party hacks.

This immigration policy will one day manifest itself in a way we're not going to like. And the day that it happens, I hope the people of this nation will remember the people who instigated it.

THE UNMOVABLE LANGUAGE BARRIER

There is a big ruckus going on nowadays about whether to teach only English in our schools. Both sides have what I'm sure are heartfelt points.

One side says that if only English is taught it will be denying the ethnic groups access to their heritage, and the other side says that because English is the first language of this nation that English should be the only language taught.

I can't see what the big fuss is about. In my mind, to allow children to go even one day in school without learning the officially spoken language of the country they live in is a cruel and unwise thing to do.

Is being able to speak Spanish or Korean going to help that child in the real world? Not unless they go back to Mexico or Korea and if they wanted to do that, what are they doing here in the first place?

And insofar as heritage goes, is it not discrimination to allow one ethnic group's language at the exclusion of all the others? Is it fair to honor the heritage of, say, kids from a Latin American background when you may have students with German, French, Arabic, or whatever backgrounds whose parents may speak the language at home but cannot speak it in the workplace?

One of the requirements for citizenship in this country is that you must learn to speak English. If this is a requirement for our immigrants, shouldn't it be a requirement for our school children?

I certainly believe that ethnic heritage is a wonderful thing and very few people are bigger on tradition than I am. I believe that people should be proud of the land their forefathers came from, but their forefathers came to this country for a better life and to truly achieve that better life speaking English is a foregone conclusion.

In an already failing school system that turns out students that can't read even the most elementary things, why should we complicate it even more by condoning something that we know beyond a shadow of a doubt is going to hurt that child when he or she tries to enter the work force?

I sometimes wonder what's behind this. I think if one were to look hard enough there is probably a political agenda hidden in there somewhere—politicians kowtowing for the minority vote. The first thing you know they will be wanting the ballots printed in multiple languages.

Though I have the greatest respect for anybody's heritage, I say let's practice that heritage at home. Schools are to educate and one of the most integral parts of that education is learning to speak and write in English.

I wonder if it would be all right to pray in school in a foreign language?

SEPARATION OF CHURCH AND STATE

There is a lot being said these days about the separation of church and state.

People tend to think that the Constitution has this provision to keep the church from exerting influence over the affairs of government.

I wonder how many people know what the Constitution actually says about separation of church and state. Well, let me enlighten you.

> *"Congress shall pass no law respecting an establishment of religion, or prohibiting the free exercise thereof, or abridging the freedom of speech or of the press, or the right of the people peaceably to assemble, and to petition the government for a redress of grievances."*

Let's break it down.

Congress shall pass no law respecting the establishment of religion, or prohibiting the free exercise thereof.

In other words, the government cannot tell us how, when, or where to worship.

Or abridging the freedom of speech, or the press.

How can the government tell schools that they cannot have a prayer before a ball game or any other time as long as it's student initiated? How can they ban Bibles or any other book for that matter? Isn't the written word a form of freedom of speech?

The media can say anything they want and no politician would dare try to limit what they say, but the rights of individuals to speak their minds is guaranteed just as strongly as the rights of the press.

Or the right of the people peaceably to assemble.

The state cannot deny the rights of any group, whatever their beliefs, to get together and discuss, criticize, or anything else they want to do.

And to petition the government for the redress of grievances.

We have a right to go to Washington and walk the halls of Congress and let our legislators know what we think about what they're doing or try to persuade them to take a favorable stand on some issue that interests us.

Does it say anywhere that religious groups should not be included in petitioning the government?

Why then do Norman Lear and the People for the American Way get apoplexy when the Christian Coalition or some other religious group lets their wishes be known to Congress? Isn't this not specifically guaranteed by the Constitution?

Does it say that the name of God should be stricken from every official document and every public place, as the ACLU wants to do? Can somebody tell me where that is in the Constitution? It's not in my copy.

BLACK WEDNESDAY

It seems that one atheist has convinced a couple of judges in California to declare the Pledge of Allegiance unconstitutional. He says that he is offended that his daughter has to be exposed to the words "one nation under God."

He says that if we said "under Buddha" or something similar that it would offend the Christian element in this country. He says that the phrase "In God We Trust" should be taken off our money.

He says that he doesn't believe in God and that God has no place in American official life.

Well, let me tell you something, you poor misguided fool, less than one second into eternity you will find out about the God you so vehemently deny the existence of. You pinheaded numbskull, do you think that your puny attempts to eradicate God from American life will succeed? Not as long as there is breath in my body. I will say "under God" when I say the pledge no matter how many idiotic judges say I can't, and if I had a child in your school district I would insist that he do too. I feel sorry for your daughter. Poor child.

This country was not founded nor even discovered, for that matter, by Buddhists nor Muslims and certainly not by atheists.

It was founded by people with Judeo-Christian beliefs whether you like it or not, and there ain't a thing you can do about it.

While I respect the right of anyone to practice whatever kind of religion they choose in this country, I readily and emphatically state that the Judeo-Christian beliefs are what made this country great.

You may say you don't believe in God but you have a god whether you want one or not. His name is Satan, and I'm sure that your god is well pleased with the despicable thing you've just done. After all, I'm sure that this plot was hatched in the bowels of hell.

This is the classic case of the tail wagging the dog. This may work with a couple of senile jurists but I will assure you that you've kicked up a hornet's nest across this country.

I am sick and tired of the majority of this nation having to live under the fear of offending a few fools who think they are wiser than Almighty God.

I'm sick and tired of politicians who listen to the squeaky wheel and pass ridiculous laws that take this country down the path of decadence and danger.

I'm sick and tired of the pompous asses who are so worried about the rights of every lunatic fringe group that comes on the scene.

I'm sick and tired of seeing our children being forced to go to schools where they can't openly mention the name of their creator.

If there has ever been a classic case for school vouchers, this is it.

American parents should demand them so they can send their children to the kind of schools where they can practice their religion, or lack of, in whatever way they so choose.

I'm sick and tired of pretending that our current conflict is anything less than a battle against radical Islam. Every war in the world, except the one in Northern Ireland, is a war between Islam and somebody.

I'm sick and tired of pretending that Saudi Arabia is a friend of ours.

Well, I will tell you one thing. You have at least one enemy and I am referring to myself and I would call on all God-fearing people in this nation to stand up and be heard, roaring loud enough so that those deaf, dumb, and blind judges can hear it way out in California.

RADICAL ISLAM

I received an e-mail from someone the other day titled, "Should we investigate Muslims?"

It was a one-sided piece with more spin than a Tom Glavine curve ball, touting Islam as a religion of peace and humanity.

While I'll admit that I don't know all there is to know about Islam, let me list some of the things I do know.

1. Over 3,000 people were slaughtered on September 11, 2001, by followers of Islam.
2. Muslims who have absolutely no regard for innocent children regularly blow up buses full of Israeli citizens.
3. Muslims in the Philippines regularly carry out kidnappings and murder.
4. The wanton murder of innocent tourists in Indonesia was carried out by Islamists.
5. The first bombing of the Trade Towers, the destruction of two of our foreign embassies, and the bombing of the U.S.S *Cole* were all done by Muslims.
6. The killing of U.S. Marines in Lebanon and the crash over Lockerbie, Scotland, were perpetrated by Muslims.
7. Women living under Islamic rule are not second- or even third-class citizens. They are treated like animals, beaten with sticks, and put to death at the whim of the authorities.

8. Islam does not allow freedom of religion, freedom of speech, nor freedom of the press. Anybody promoting any other faith is subjected to harsh punishment and anybody criticizing Islam could be convicted of blasphemy and put to death.
9. Almost every shooting war on this planet is between Islam and somebody.

And the list could go on and on, but I'm sure you get the drift. If Islam is such a peaceful religion, why do they refuse to denounce the violence and denial of human rights?

Even some of the Islamic clergy in America advocate the overthrow of this nation.

I know that some of you are going to counter what I've said by saying that some of the worst atrocities on earth have been done in the name of Christianity. I know this to be true and vehemently denounce every incident from the Spanish Inquisition to the present-day cult activity. None of these things represent true Christianity. The present-day Christian church also denounces them.

But until I see the majority of the practitioners of Islam step forward and fully denounce the violence and carnage that is done in the name of their religion, save your "Islam is a peaceful religion" e-mails.

It just doesn't ring true.

A DANGEROUS PRECEDENT

The Supreme Court set a dangerous precedent this past week when they ruled that the PGA had to allow Casey Martin to ride in a golf cart to compete in professional golf tournaments.

Casey Martin has a physical disability which prevents him from walking between the holes.

I want to preface my remarks by saying that I have nothing against Casey Martin nor any other physically handicapped person and I admire anybody who goes against the odds and accomplishes something above and beyond, despite their physical disabilities.

I personally don't have a problem with Casey Martin or anybody else riding in a golf cart. The senior players are allowed to use golf carts if they want to, which almost all of them decline. I don't think the use of golf carts would destroy professional golf or hurt it in any significant way.

But that's really not the point. The point is does our government—judicial branch, executive branch, or legislative branch—have the right to tell private organizations what they must and must not do?

I also happen to think that the PGA is at times a stuffy, high-handed outfit and certainly don't agree with everything they do. But if they say their players must walk the golf course there should be no exceptions. It's up to that august organization to decide the rules of professional golf, and if someone doesn't like it there is no law which prevents them from starting their own outfit and making the rules any way they want to.

Government intervention in private life is a very dangerous thing. They never have enough power and, unchecked, will be telling you how many times you can go to the bathroom a day.

Don't laugh: Out of control, power hungry government is an awesome thing.

The government in China even tells people how many children they can have and mandates abortion for those who go over the limit.

What if a one armed man wants to play baseball, or a blind man wants to play soccer. Will the Supreme Court step in and say that they have to be allowed to play regardless of their disability? Can you see where this could lead?

I know that the government comes on like the big benevolent daddy who wants to take care of everybody, but in reality it is, for the most part, a bunch of power hungry men and women who think they can spend our hard-earned money better than we can, raise our children better than we can and control private enterprise better than we can. When the truth is told, they can't even run themselves. They can't balance a budget, they can't run a post office which is as efficient as private carriers, they don't manufacture anything, and in my opinion, they act like a bunch of spoiled third-graders most of the time.

On the other hand, the PGA has been successful for many years, makes its own money, gives great entertainment to the citizens of this country, and has no trouble balancing its budget. It's self-sufficient, self-proliferating, and we don't have to listen to them whine every time we turn on a television set.

Maybe it should be the other way around; maybe the PGA should be telling the U.S. government how to clean up its act.

FAT POWER

I do believe that I heard the most ridiculous thing on television the other night that I've ever heard. They are trying to pass a law in San Francisco to prevent discrimination against fat people.

Where does this junk stop? What's next—short people, people with pimples, left-handed people, people who wear glasses? This political correctness trash is silly and serves only to turn this nation into a bunch of lily-livered, pantywaist, limp-wristed, soft-spoken milksops that can be herded around like a bunch of sheep by politicians with the morals of an alley cat.

The recently passed hate laws are an example of a society slowly slipping into semantical lunacy.

I think that if you murder anyone it's a pretty good sign that you hate that person whether they be straight or gay, black or white, fat or skinny. Why do we need another law when we don't enforce the ones we have on the books now?

The same crowd of dubious do-gooders who scream for hate laws and such are the first ones to pitch a fit at the mere mention of enforcing the death penalty.

These people literally make me sick. They'll go to any lengths to save a baby seal but won't lift a finger to save an unborn child. They'll get out in the streets and march for "women's rights" but when a woman not of their political persuasion, i.e., Paula Jones, gets wronged they turn a blind eye and a deaf ear.

They castigate the Jim Bakers of this world while supporting a lying president who can't keep his fly zipped up, even in the Oval Office.

They scream about gays not being able to serve in the military they don't even support.

If this nation doesn't get some kind of moral leadership and if these people continue to dominate the media and politics, what will this nation turn into?

We'll just have to stop talking to each other for fear we'll say something that's against the law. You won't be able to criticize anything.

Can you just imagine what's going to happen when the liberal politicians have raised their vote buying social programs until there are more non-productive people than productive people?

When the majority of the people are on the dole and the hard-working men and women of this nation can no longer bear the burden of this runaway train?

When there's no one left to pick the cotton, and not enough tax money to go around, when some gay person sues the military before some bleeding heart judge and tears our fighting forces all to pieces? When our prisons get so full that we don't have anywhere to incarcerate the criminals? When you have to traverse our city streets in an armored vehicle? When our slowly disappearing liberties have gone away like school prayer?

Wake up, America. I'll say it again. Wake up, America!!!! The hard-working, God-fearing people of this nation have got to stand up and be heard.

I pray for America. I pray to the very God who has been treated so poorly in our nation. He is a merciful God or else this country would have already gone the way of Sodom and Gomorrah.

ENOUGH ALREADY

Zell Miller, the governor of the great and beautiful state of Georgia, recently stood up in front of the state legislature and then played an excerpt from Beethoven's "Ode to Joy."

Now I think that makes a whole lot more sense than a lot of things that happen in state legislatures, and I, for one, believe that a little Beethoven never hurt anybody.

The problem is that the honorable governor was proposing that the state of Georgia pass out CDs of this admittedly wonderful music to the parents of every child blessed enough to be born in Georgia from now on. The reason being that if this music was played to the infants in the formative years it would increase their capacity to absorb book learning, and I'm sure there's an outside chance that he may be right. After all, who am I, a lowly fiddle player, to be questioning the expertise of the governor of the sovereign state of Georgia?

It's not his belief that I'm questioning, it's the downright ridiculous notion that the taxpayers of his state should foot the bill for a bunch of CDs that are probably going to get tossed in the corner with the junk mail and never even opened, much less played.

I mean, come on, Governor, do you really think that the people who honestly believe that classical music is going to improve their children's lives would not be willing to spend twelve dollars or so to buy it?

Have we become so dependent on government in this country that we have to let them tell us what kind of music to play for our babies? To go so far as supplying it? I think not.

What comes next? Will you be telling us what kind of formula to feed them, maybe one with some kind of brain food in it?

Why can't you people get it through your heads that that is not what government is supposed to be about? It's none of the government's business how we raise our children.

Speaking for myself, I think your time would be better spent trying to get the kids off crack instead of trying to get them on classical music. How about creating an atmosphere of discipline and respect in our schools? Wouldn't that be more beneficial to learning that Beethoven?

Mrs. Hillary Clinton wrote a book a while back called, "It Takes A Village," implying that we need help raising our kids.

No, Mrs. Clinton, it doesn't take a village. It just takes a family.

THE FALLACY OF LEGALIZING DRUGS

There is quite a move afoot these days amongst those of a more liberal bent to solve our pandemic drug problem by making them legal.

Of course it's the same old, "save the whales" and "kill the babies," "don't enforce the immigration laws," "if you can't beat 'em, join 'em" crowd of pseudo-intellectual pea brains who tell us on the one hand that you can't legislate morals and on the other that you can legislate away our drug problem.

It's hard to believe that even this crowd of elite busybodies, who are absolutely aghast at the very thought of school children being exposed to a sign on the wall saying, *Thou shalt not kill*, could be foggy enough to believe that legalizing drugs would do anything to solve our problem.

First of all, in my mind I have serious moral objections to the proposition. Making it legal doesn't make it right and actually goes so far as to say it's all right to do drugs as long as you're old enough to buy them. We can't even keep nicotine and alcohol out of the hands of the young. How do they expect to keep legal drugs away from them.

But let's forget the moral issue for a moment and just look at the practical side. Who would run this program? Why, the good old, dependable, incorrupt, and efficient federal government, of course.

The same people who brought you such hits as the Internal Revenue Service.

Can you imagine the monolithic monster of bureaucracy these dingalings would put into place to administer this great hope of mankind?

They could call it the Internal National Service for Narcotics Enforcement and the acronym could be INSANE, because that's just about what this program would amount to.

Alcohol and tobacco are the most taxed commodities on the market. This is called a sin tax. Can you imagine what would happen every time our benevolent Congress would want to implement one of its "Let's get the vote out" social programs?

That's right; they'd raise the taxes on drugs, making them cost so much that they could not possibly compete with the illegal drugs on the street.

So the incentive of taking the profit out of dealing would be gone.

So where is the rationale for this grand design? Some will tell you that Holland has tried the experiment successfully. Not so, Holland tried the experiment, all right, but it was not successful. It creates more problems than it solves.

But I'm not worried about this issue getting serious, at least not under this administration. After all, the elections are just around the corner and Colombia has plenty of money to donate to political campaigns.

FARMERS

The most indispensable segment of our society has got to be our farmers. Our very existence depends on them. Food, clothing, medicine, and any number of other things are produced by them.

And yet, with all the importance they hold in the economy and well-being of this nation they are one of the most put-upon and disregarded industries in existence.

I'm not speaking about the big corporate monstrosities that control thousands and thousands of acres and gobble up the government subsidies which were probably put into place for their benefit anyway.

I'm referring to one of the original institutions of free enterprise, the family farm, the guy with a few acres and a desire to grow things.

It seems that business and our government to some extent have conspired to do away with the family farm. And what a shame. There is no better way of life if you are acclimated to it. It's hard work, but one of the most honest and rewarding professions a person can have.

We import products which are government-subsidized and produced by cheap labor while the family farmer sits and wonders just how much longer he can hold off the bank.

Our politicians send billions of dollars to corrupt governments, a large part of which ends up in Swiss bank accounts instead of feeding the starving population.

We export technology to nations that will use it to our detriment. We prop up dictatorships and prolong suffering by meddling in the foreign affairs of nations that only want our money.

Well, I've got an idea. Instead of sending money and technology why don't we send food and clothing? Food can't be deposited in the bank and clothing can't be put in a missile and fired back at us.

Instead of paying our farmers to let their fields lie fallow, why not put them into full production and feed and clothe the underprivileged nations of the world?

Television is inundated with pictures of pitiful children and the mothers and fathers who are powerless to take care of them, and I for one am deeply affected by these images, which most of the time have been caused by a heartless administration more concerned with holding on to power than feeding its starving masses.

Enough! Why shouldn't we feed these helpless people? Why shouldn't we clothe them? Why shouldn't we send food instead of money, clothes instead of bullets, and medicine instead of technology?

No matter how much military hardware, technology, and money we send to these people they are always going to be anti-American.

But who can hate you for feeding them? Who can be against you when you supply the medicine that saves the lives of their children and who can speak against you when you put clothes on their back?

Our family farms and ranches could be prospering as well as the satellite business which does business with our farmers.

I'm sure that if you approached a Washington politician with this idea he would say, "You just don't understand, it's just not that simple," to which I would reply, "How could you possibly know if you haven't tried it?"

ECO TERRORISTS

Somehow I cannot find the least bit of justice nor the least bit of sanity in destroying someone else's property for some cause.

Case in point, what does the burning of SUVs have to do with the saving of the environment? Truth be known, the bunch of eco kooks who burned a sales lot full of SUVs last week in Eugene, Oregon, did more harm to the environment in a couple of hours than the exhaust from these vehicles would have done for quite a while, all that rubber and paint releasing their toxic fumes into the air.

These people are completely off the wall and should be dealt with harshly. If they are let go they will be off on a tangent and there's no telling where it will end. Will they start murdering people whose views differ from theirs?

Will they start blowing up power plants? Will they start sabotaging airplanes and derailing locomotives and anything else that doesn't fit their bigoted and fascist-like view of the way things should be?

They are simply trying to force their views on the rest of the population and doing so by force, and if our politicians have one ounce of brainpower, which I doubt sometimes, they'll make an all-out effort to nip this in the bud and put these people behind bars where they belong.

The logging industry has been plagued with these people for many years in their misguided quest to save the spotted owl.

What makes me sick more than anything else about these people is that they are willing to cause all kinds of misery to save a bird that most of us never knew existed, and would not raise a finger to stop the slaughter of unborn children.

If these people have their way, there will be one national park from the Atlantic to the Pacific, the country would be plunged into darkness when all the electricity being produced by coal, oil, and nuclear energy would be shut off, industry would grind to a standstill. The farmers would have to stop producing food and the military would cease to exist.

California has already found out the folly of giving in to these radicals and is experiencing blackouts and other inconveniences caused by not allowing the building of power plants and the exploration of other energy sources.

Now, before some of you left-wing watchdogs get your poison pens out, let me say a couple of things.

First of all, I care passionately about the environment and I take care of my little piece of the earth. I don't even throw a gum wrapper on the ground, and yes, I'm even kind to wild animals. Just ask the raccoons who eat the leftover food out of my dog's bowl on the back porch, or the wild turkeys who roam my barnyard or the white-tailed deer who graze my pastures and gracefully jump my fences.

I learned about taking care of the environment from an expert, my dad, who made his living in the timber business. The timberlands he harvested bore new trees decade after decade because they were managed properly. Nature and man were served because of his knowledge and compassion for the forests of his beloved pine trees, and I love the woods and waters as much as any man.

I just happen to think that man can live in harmony with nature. God gave us this planet to subdue and make our living, and yes, to take care of. But taking care of it and being militantly megalomaniacal about it are two different things.

I'll take care of the planet but I'll also take care of my property, and I'll tell you what, the first SOB who burns my SUV is going to get a .357 in his butt.

GASOLINE PRICES

You can't get away from the gas pump anymore without shelling out major bucks, which just infuriates me.

It doesn't matter what the U.S.A. does for other countries, they never seem to appreciate it. As in the case of Saudi Arabia, when we put our sons and daughters in harm's way to liberate them from Saddam Hussein. It just didn't seem to matter when it came to squeezing us for more oil money.

There's an old adage that says we either learn from history or we are doomed to repeat it.

Well, we should have learned back in the seventies just how ruthless and uncaring these people are.

What ever happened to ethanol and all the other grandiose plans for synthetic fuels which were supposed to take us out of the clutches of the Arabs and be much better for the environment? Where are you when we need you, Al Gore?

I hear people say that we still don't pay as much for fuel as they do in Europe. Well, I don't give a flip what Europe does about their gas—pardon me, petrol prices. I don't want to spend the rent every time I want to drive around the block.

Who is going to do something about this situation? Of course, I know Bill Clinton won't or probably can't. I don't know of even one foreign situation he has prevailed in.

The Congress will probably try but by the time they get through straining a bill through the two-party sieve it probably wouldn't mean anything anyway, and it would probably have so many pork codicils attached to it that it would look like a New York City yellow pages.

So if we're going to be stuck with these kinds of oil prices I have a few suggestions:

Let's get back to that artificial fuel thing. Since it is plant-based it would do wonders for our farmers.

Let's cut any kind of aid, military or otherwise, which we are giving to the OPEC nations.

Let's open up the capped wells in Oklahoma and Texas so that our domestic economy can reap some of the benefits.

Let's buy more oil from Mexico and South America and everywhere else in the world where it's available and wean ourselves off Middle Eastern oil.

Let's face the facts, folks. One of these days there is going to be a hardcore shooting war in that part of the world and our oil supply is going to be cut off indefinitely, so we may as well go and do something about it while we can.

I, for one, am getting tired of paying for the mistakes of our politicians over and over again. We should have been stockpiling oil when the price was at its lowest. If we had, we could now fall back on that reserve and wait OPEC out. It wouldn't take but a couple of weeks, a month at the most in my opinion, before they would be begging to sell us their oil at reasonable prices.

Hit 'em where it hurts, in the pocketbook. After all, turn about is fair play.

SHOULD WE REPEAL NAFTA?

Before I begin this article I would like to make you all aware of something. It came to my attention not long ago that a lot of the merchandise we were using, tee shirts, caps, etc., was coming from foreign countries. I instructed my people to sell off the foreign merchandise and that from now on all our products would be American made.

While this is not possible in the case of some specialty items our mainstream products are available from American companies and will be purchased from them.

Now the article.

Recently I read an astute and extremely well-written piece on the North American Free Trade Agreement (NAFTA), which is a trade agreement between the U.S.A., Canada, and Mexico.

It was supposed to expedite trade between the three nations and be beneficial to all three economies by tearing down barriers and facilitating the flow of goods across international borders.

I have heard a lot of people whom I respect say that NAFTA is a good thing. Good for who? I'll tell you who: a handful of power-grabbing corporations and international financiers.

Since its inception in 1994, NAFTA has eliminated somewhere around 800,000 jobs in the U.S.A.

Remember that giant sucking sound Ross Perot talked about?

Armed with the threat of moving industries to Mexico, these modern-day robber barons take advantage of an already beleaguered labor force.

Another sad thing is that NAFTA hasn't done very much for the economies of Canada and Mexico, although they have benefited considerably more than the U.S.A.

Why and how did this happen? While I'm sure there were many well-intentioned people involved at the beginning, I feel that NAFTA was designed and orchestrated to line the pockets of a lot of people who are already incredibly rich.

It seems there is an element in this country which is determined to lead us down the primrose path of economic deception.

Enron, WorldCom, and several other companies cooked the books and cheated their employees and stockholders while the top executives made off with decadent fortunes.

I feel that the NAFTA agreement somewhat parallels these debacles, insofar as deception is concerned.

It's time we took a long look at NAFTA. Is it really beneficial to the masses or only to the super-rich? Is it good for the work force or is it an underhanded, union breaking tactic to drive down labor costs and add to the all consuming bottom line?

It seems that every time we give up our sovereignty, whether it be to the United Nations or to international business interests, our fingers get severely burned.

I will be the first one to admit that I'm not a globalist. I believe in the sovereignty of nations, the right to defend themselves, militarily or economically.

There is now another fiasco on the drawing board called the FTAA, the Free Trade Agreement of the Americas, which includes North, Central, and South America. I think you can probably make an educated guess at what the outcome of this would be. It would certainly move more industries south, taking jobs with them.

The power of a nation should not be centered in the hands of a few elite industrialists. What ever happened to "We the people"?

FISCAL RESPONSIBILITY

Did you ever stop to think that every time you buy a gallon of gasoline or go through a toll booth or buy a license that you're paying taxes?

Did you realize that when you die, if you have accumulated a significant amount of wealth, the federal government can take the lion's share of money you have already paid the taxes on at one time?

We are all aware of the income taxes we are burdened with, but I don't believe that most people are aware of the hidden taxes we pay without even thinking about them.

Another thing that I don't believe we consciously think about is that our elected leaders work for us. We are not their slaves nor their employees, and we are not constitutionally bound to supply all the money they can waste on their pork barrel projects and ill-advised whims.

The way that it should work is that we should give them an amount of money to run the government on and they should have to stay within a budget. If they can't run the government on what we allow them, then they should be fired.

In the first place, the bureaucracy has reached gigantic proportions on federal and state levels. Political patronage and downright sloth have allowed this bloated giant to reach the level that it takes around 70 cents out of every dollar we send to Washington just to maintain the status quo.

If you've ever had any dealings with the federal government you know just how inefficient it can be. Any private business operated in the same fashion would not last a year in a competitive market.

The motivation in Washington, in most cases, is not to serve the people, it is to be able to get enough votes to be reelected. Which, in my book, demonstrates a screaming need for term limits.

The politicians talk about campaign finance reform but nobody really does anything about it because it works to their advantage and they don't want to see it reformed.

They talk about taxing the rich, making them pay their fair share, when what they really mean is, "We want more money to spend to buy votes."

Taxing the rich is not the windfall the politicians would have you believe. The money that the wealthy pay into the bottomless federal coffers is the same money they would otherwise put into investments, creating jobs and prosperity.

I believe that everyone should pay their fair share, but what I think a lot of people don't realize is that a tax on anybody shakes out to be a tax on everybody in one way or another.

Bill Clinton takes credit for an economy that started a comeback when Ronald Reagan cut taxes and put in place other fiscally beneficial policies which were reaching fruition about the time that Clinton came into office.

The Democratic platform is nothing more than a wish list of more socialistic programs which in one way or another every American will pay for in the long run.

I don't know about you, but I hate socialism, I don't want a one world government, and I couldn't care less what other countries energy policies are.

This is the United States of America, conceived in liberty, dedicated to freedom, and paid for in blood.

We are one nation, under God, no matter how many times the ACLU goes to court to try to prove otherwise.

I don't mind paying taxes, but I'm sick and tired of paying for the useless pet projects of a bunch of irresponsible politicians.

They strut and posture, they cajole and criticize, they claim to feel our pain.

But in the end all their carrying on is, as the Bard so aptly put it, sound and fury signifying nothing.

GIVING IN

Well, the International Olympic Committee has done it again. After the fiasco over the Salt Lake City winter games they've turned around and done something even more appalling by awarding the 2008 games to Red China (emphasis on red).

Aren't the games supposed to be about the best and highest ideals, fair play, and honor?

If so, then how can these people allow the games to go to a country with state-sanctioned suppression of speech and any kind of personal freedom, run by a bunch of hoodlums who just happen to have all the guns?

What is it with these people? Are these not the liberal elite who scream the loudest about human rights? This is hypocrisy of the highest order.

I wouldn't give them the time of day, the bunch of depraved butchers.

What about the detainment of American citizens who visit China? What about the prisons full of political prisoners who had the audacity to utter a word against the scumbag tyrants who run the country? What about the forced abortions, the persecution of Christians, the stifling of personal initiative, and the never-ending physical abuse of dissidents?

By giving the games to China the International Olympic Committee is helping legitimize the most repressive regime since Joseph Stalin.

I heard something to the effect that if China didn't get the games that they would be mad and take it out on the United States. In other words, they are holding the world hostage because they're afraid that the Chinese are going to raise some hell.

Well, I say, let them raise all the hell they want to. I say, hold their feet to the fire. If they want to join the civilized world then it's high time they started acting like a civilized country instead of a bunch of out-of-control warlords with a billion people to push around.

Let them rant and rave, threaten and posture. As much as business people in this country would try to convince you otherwise, we don't need the Red Chinese or anything they produce. They are the ones who need us. They need our technology and our know-how to help bring them into the twenty-first century. They need our resources and hardware to bring them out of the Middle Ages.

Are these not the same people who systematically stole our

nuclear technology and corrupted our election process by contributing mass amounts of money to the Clinton-Gore campaign?

Are these not the people who rattle their sabers the loudest and the most often, who thumb their collective nose when the rest of the world protests their barbaric behavior?

Shame on you, International Olympic Committee, shame on you for your cowardice, for your greed, and for turning your back on the world's biggest population who suffer at the hands of the very people who are going to profit from the games.

I don't know what you could have been thinking about but it certainly wasn't freedom and justice for all.

Who's next, Cuba?

TORT REFORM

For years now the Congress has been talking about tort reform legislation, a bill to limit collectable damages in certain types of lawsuits.

The lawyers are up in arms about it and have their propaganda machine in full throttle trying to convince the public that limiting liability would not be fair to the injured parties.

Well, that dog just won't hunt. I believe the truth of the matter is that the law would limit the amount of fees the lawyers could collect and that's what they're so upset about. If they're so concerned about the welfare of their clients why do they often take the lion's share of class action lawsuit settlements? Why don't they let most of the money go to the parties who deserve it, the ones who have been harmed?

And let me here enter a caveat. I don't believe that all lawyers are money-grubbing opportunists; there are good and honest lawyers too. And don't get the impression that I am against people suing for legitimate grievances.

But I know for a fact that there are attorneys out there who try to persuade people to sue whether they are hurt or not, just to make someone pay; and getting hundreds of thousands of dollars for spilling coffee in your lap is way beyond the pale.

We've all read about the silly lawsuits and the unbelievable amounts of money that have been paid out. We laugh at the foolishness because it sounds like a joke. The sad fact is that it is not a joke. Did you ever stop to think that every dollar these unprincipled attorneys can persuade a jury to award their clients has to be made up by somebody?

That's right, folks, and guess who that somebody is? We the people, you and me and all the other hard-working unsuspecting stiffs out there.

We pay it in higher insurance premiums, higher consumer prices, and higher medical costs.

Medical malpractice insurance prices are spiraling out of control and if something isn't done soon the day could come when small towns in America could lose most if not all of their quality physicians.

Of course, some of the blame for the medical debacle has to be laid at the door of the American Medical Association. Their failure to properly police their profession and their reluctance to take away the license of the incompetent who practice under their auspices are the source of a lot of the trouble.

Of course, the same could be said for the American Bar Association. There would be a lot more respect for their profession if they would purge their ranks of these ambulance chasers and establish some guidelines on their own.

As rampant as the problem is, and as aware as Congress is of the situation, I seriously doubt if politicians have the guts to pass meaningful tort reform legislation for two reasons:

First, it's the money-heavy legal profession lobby, and second, what is Congress made up of? That's right: mostly lawyers.

We're going to find out in the next few months who the government cares the most about, the ordinary people of the United States or a bunch of greedy, unprincipled lawyers who care nothing for the trouble they're causing as long as it fattens their bank accounts.

Love of money truly is the root of all evil.

SOME THOUGHTS ON NAPSTER

I have been asked what I think about Napster, the online music pirates, and I would like to answer all those who inquired and also those of you who didn't just to let you all know where I stand on this issue.

Napster practiced larceny pure and simple, because they took somebody else's property and made it available to the general public for free.

I know that this is hard for people not dealing in what is known as intellectual property (recordings, written word, etc.) to understand because there is not a tangible item. A song cannot be touched, it can only be listened to and felt, therefore it doesn't seem to be a real commercial product.

But the truth is that a song is just as much of a product to the songwriter as an automobile is to General Motors. It's a songwriter's stock in trade, just as the records are the recording artist's stock in trade, and if someone takes their means of making a living and gives it away for free just because they can, it's tantamount to stealing.

Intellectual property has always been hard to protect. Due to ignorance and apathy in our legislative bodies, the laws governing the protection of intellectual property have always lagged behind new technologies, leaving unscrupulous characters free to pirate and exploit the people who create the music until the government finally gets around to doing something about it, and by then untold millions of dollars are lost forever.

One of the e-mails I received asked what Napster was doing that wasn't already being done by the taping of movies off television. The answer is that the fee for using the movie has already been paid before it's shown on TV. With Napster, there is no fee.

The best way I know to explain the situation is in hypothetical terms. Let's say that you owned a grocery store and that every day somebody would come by and load up a truck full of bread, meat, butter, etc., took it out on the street outside your door, and gave it away to anyone who had gumption enough to walk up and take it—and there was absolutely nothing you could do about it.

Not only would you lose the money on the groceries they took, how many people do you think would come into your store and buy your wares when they were readily available for free just outside your door?

That's what Napster was doing to the music business, not just the artists and songwriters, but to the record companies, the pressing plants, the retail outlets, and the trucking companies who haul the product from manufacturer to record stores.

And any number of little people up and down the line who actually have nothing to do with the music business.

So you see, Napster is exactly what the name implies, thieves pure and simple who in the long run could do serious damage to the creation and recording of music.

WHATEVER HAPPENED TO THE MUSIC?

Maybe I'm a little oversensitive about the subject of music. After all, I've made my living in the music business for over forty years. It's taken me places I'd never have gone without it. It's given me things that I never would have had without it.

It's worked me hard and kept me away from my family for long periods of time, but the rewards have been gratifying, and not just from a monetary standpoint but by being able to spend my life doing something I dearly love.

I have a deep and abiding respect for the music business, and when I say music business I am referring to the creation and performance of music. That's my part of it.

It hurts me when I see it being invaded by a bunch of bean counting, ruthless, totally profit-motivated bozos with dollar signs in their eyes and a mercenary attitude toward music in their hearts.

Many of the major radio stations in this nation are programmed by a handful of tin-eared tyrants called consultants. They are not happy with slowly killing country music. Now they want to start charging record companies for playing their records.

Oh, they try to use other terms to describe it, but that's what it comes down to, play for pay. Whatever happened to payola? I thought it was illegal.

And besides, the airwaves of this nation do not belong to a handful of greedy individuals who program radio stations. They belong to we, the people. They are for our entertainment, education, and for keeping us informed.

I think it's disgraceful for radio stations to charge to play records. After all, is that not biting the hand that feeds it?

If there were no records to play there would be no music radio and therefore these people would be out of a job.

I don't know if the general public realizes what is happening or not, but the U.S. government has deregulated radio stations, which on the surface sounds good.

But in reality what it boils down to is that one of these days, and it's arriving fast, most of the major media in this country will be in the hands of three or four powerful cartels who can attempt to mold public opinion at will.

They're already doing it with music; wait until they start with politics.

What's going to happen is that these people are going to gather so much power around themselves that there won't be but a smidgen of politicians who would risk their wrath by trying to do something about it.

It's funny to me that our government gives up control of our nation's airwaves and then turns around and tries to tell us how to raise our children.

I view this as a very dangerous situation with dire possibilities for a lot more than the music business.

Whatever happened to music being played on the radio just because it was good and not because some Perrier-swilling number cruncher thinks it fits a certain image?

Whatever happened to the concept that if the people in Lafayette like a record who cares whether the people in Peoria like it or not, and vice versa?

Whatever happened to commitment and caring? Whatever happened to the music?

TRASHYVISION

Evidently everybody is not as bored, unentertained, and downright disgusted by what they see on television these days as I am or there would be some major changes made pronto.

Sitcoms that promote profanity and sex, talk shows that exploit the lowest instincts of humankind, and slanted news reporting, in my opinion, have turned the silver screen into the slimy screen.

Sally Jesse Raphael, Ricky Lake, and Jerry Springer expose us to the dark side of troubled people while Howard Stern doesn't even pay lip service to decency.

Sitting and watching the sitcom drivel is just a few notches lower than getting a root canal done, and if I see one more infomercial I think I'm going to throw up.

OK, one judge was fun, and two judges were tolerable, but this is getting ridiculous. There's even a judge for animals now. There's even a channel for people who can't get enough of Judge Judy and her ilk.

And the awards shows, did you ever see the like? There's the Academy Awards, the American Music Awards, the Country Music Association Awards, the Academy of Country Music Awards, the Emmy Awards, the Grammy Awards, and on and on and on. I guess there'll be an awards show honoring the best award shows before it's over.

The language on TV is only exceeded in vulgarity by the plots of the shows it is used on. The network news is inundated with people spouting off about the evil of guns and how they should be completely banned while the shows which follow an hour or two later on are areas of dark and bloody ground where cruelty and violence reign supreme.

At almost any public event you'll see television stars wearing little red ribbons supporting AIDS research while the shows they star on promote gratuitous sex and homosexuality.

Even the cartoons these days are full of dark figures with supernatural powers and questionable morals.

I would be remiss if I didn't state the fact that there is still some good television out there, especially during football season. And I enjoy *The O'Reilly Factor* on Fox and that Australian nut on *Animal Planet* who handles deadly snakes like they were toys.

The golf tournaments are great and of course there's Braves baseball, but those things aside, unless you happen to run across the occasional decent movie, it's teletrash and Oprah wannabes.

Now I'm not saying that we should go back to the days of *Father Knows Best* and *Leave It to Beaver*, but when I can pick up the remote and go through a hundred or so channels and not find one thing that I really want to watch either there's something wrong with TV or something wrong with me.

On such occasions I usually just turn the television set off, pick up a good book, and find myself thoroughly entertained.

Maybe that should tell me something. After all, books have been around a heck of a lot longer than television.

You've got to dedicate yourself entirely if you want to make it in the music business. Here I am in the 1960s (left, with glasses and my guitar), with one of my first bands, the Jaguars.

The Charlie Daniels Band, 2002. Left to right: Bruce Brown, Pat McDonald, me, Taz DiGregorio, Charlie Hayward, Mark Matejka

Performing with hard rock legend Ted Nugent at the Charlie Daniels Band Volunteer Jam in 1985

Recording *Self Portrait* in 1969 with Bob Dylan (left) and Fred Carter (center)

On the set of the movie *Urban Cowboy*. Left to right: Taz DiGregorio, Fred Edwards, myself, John Travolta, Jim Marshall, Charlie Hayward

Sean Hannity (left) and Alan Colmes invited me on the Fox News Channel's *Hannity & Colmes* show in 2001 to talk about the controversy generated by my song "This Ain't No Rag, It's a Flag."

I've long admired the Reverend Billy Graham and have enjoyed participating in the Billy Graham Crusades, such as this one in North Carolina in 1996.

With Dolly Parton at the fiftieth anniversary of WIVK radio in Knoxville, Tennessee, 2003

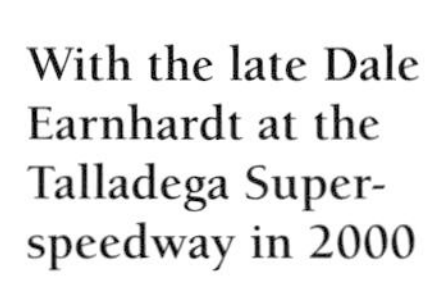

With the late Dale Earnhardt at the Talladega Superspeedway in 2000

Meeting four U.S. presidents (here I am with Ronald Reagan) was quite a thrill for this North Carolina fiddle player.

With President George H. W. Bush and country singer Travis Tritt in 1995

Greeting President Jimmy Carter and Vice President Walter Mondale at the White House

Hazel (right) and I with President Gerald Ford and former First Lady Betty Ford at his 1992 golf tournament

With Hazel and Little Charlie in front of our house in 1980

With my beautiful bride, Hazel, in 1963

I was honored to meet the head of U.S. Central Command, General Tommy Franks, and his wife Cathy (above) at MacDill Air Force Base in January, 2003.

And it was also my honor to perform for the troops at Guantanamo Bay in Cuba in March, 2002.

Performing at The Angelus in Hudson, Florida. The Angelus is a home for severely handicapped persons who are not able to care for themselves, and one of the most genuine examples of love I've ever seen.

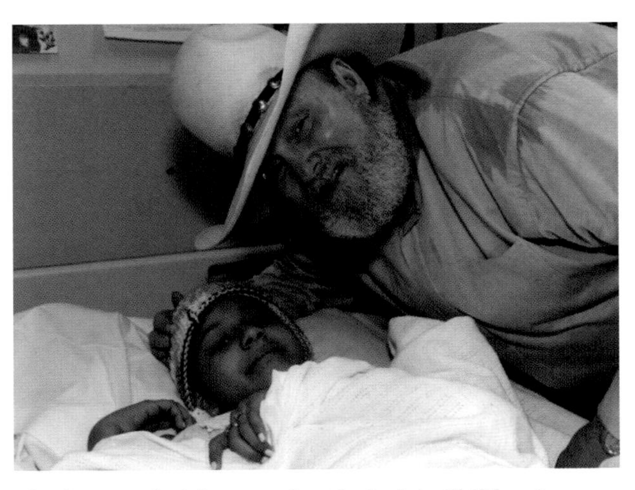

The boys and girls treated at St. Jude's Children's Research Hospital in Memphis, Tennessee, are in the best of hands, and I'm honored to serve on its professional advisory board.

GREED

The last time Major League baseball went on strike I almost lost interest in a sport I've been following all my life. I was so incensed to think that these millionaire players who live in a world that few on this earth will ever know, would turn their greedy backs on the millions of fans who have to watch their pennies just to pay the inflated price for a ticket to a game.

No playoffs, no World Series, no climax to the abbreviated season, and that's like taking a bath with your clothes on. One good thing came out of the strike, however. I learned, as I'm sure many other Americans did, that I can live without baseball if they go on strike. This year baseball could well fade into the mish-mash of soccer, arena football, and other such sports with limited audience and TV coverage. One could say it would be poetic justice, this killing off of the golden goose by a bunch of spoiled, overpaid little boys who are no longer motivated by their love of the game, but by greed and petulance.

In recent days we have watched corporate fat cats put into handcuffs and carted off to jail. These arrogant pigs, and that's what they are in my book, ran their companies into bankruptcy, lining their own pockets to the tune of more millions than they would spend in their miserable lifetimes. They put thousands of hard-working people out of jobs and drained the savings plans that their employees had planned on having to see them through their golden years. They have fostered a nervousness in the stock market, causing even the stable companies with honest executives to be distrusted by those who would invest their hard-earned money in the market. They have decimated retirement portfolios and 401k plans held by good people who have worked all their lives only to find that their retirement money has been eaten up by these greedy leeches.

What should we do about it? I say we take every cent these culprits have stolen, everything they have, in fact, their stocks and bonds, their limousines, their mansions, their corporate jets, their crystal martini pitchers, and their gold cigar lighters. Take it, sell it, and divide the money among the employees they defrauded.

The government has finally decided to make some effort at prosecution but as usual it's a day late and a dollar short, closing the barn door after the horse is in the next county. But I guess better late than never.

The problem with baseball, big business, and so many other things in America, and the world, for that matter, is nothing but pure old evil, hell-inspired greed. The "let me get mine" and "the heck with you" attitude which permeates this nation from the board room to the locker room.

It's greed that makes the drug dealer sell his poison to twelve-year-old kids, it's greed that makes the mechanic pad the repair bill, it's greed that motivates some lowlife to charge an old person way too much to fix their roof or pave their driveway. It's greed that causes manufacturers to use inferior components in their products. It's greed that causes a board of directors to put so much pressure on their executives that they sacrifice their honor and integrity just to add a few points to the almighty bottom line.

For too long corporate raiding and buying companies just to split them up for profit with no thought of the effects on long-time employees has been accepted as the norm in this country.

When cold-hearted executives fire a person just before they are eligible for retirement benefits, it's nothing short of stealing.

I believe in capitalism. I believe in making money and getting ahead in life, but not by stepping on the heads of other people. It's not necessary to hurt other people to get ahead. It's possible to conduct your business treating your employees and your consumers fairly. It may not pay as well but at least you can sleep at night.

GRAFFITI

If there is a written advertisement heralding the rapid decay of our society in my opinion it is graffiti.

There is no escaping the stuff. Whether on the sides of subway cars in New York City or a bridge abutment in lower Alabama, it glowers at us in its Day-Glo arrogance, this ugly, useless, illegible reminder of just how far we've fallen on the decency scale.

Those who practice this insanity have no respect for people, property, nor the common good. They spray-paint their filth on the sides of public buildings and private property with no regard for the rights of their fellow man.

The most disturbing thing about graffiti is that it is being accepted as part of life in America, just another notation on the growing list of things that we can't do anything about.

When I was a kid a bunch of high school boys got the bright idea that they would throw paint on a local drive-in and teenage hangout. Of course they were caught and their sentence was that they had to cover all the paint they had thrown on the building. Not hire it done, but to do it with their own hands.

The public humiliation alone was enough to induce considerable remorse in these misled young men, not to mention the manual labor required.

Now, in my opinion, the judge who passed this sentence was extremely wise. He forced these kids to undo what they had done, to right the wrong, in other words, to be responsible for their own actions. He didn't let them off with a slap on the wrist and he didn't let them fall back on Daddy's money. His idea was you broke it now you fix it and in the full view of those you offended.

I only wish that every graffiti writer in this country could be caught and made to scrub every molecule of this disgusting eyesore off whatever surface they had chosen to deface. I think our graffiti problem would go away in about two weeks.

The youth of today are coddled and spoiled by a system that believes, or at least pretends to believe that every act of malice is caused by some ulterior influence, some quirk of the environment, something far beyond the youth's realm of control, so therefore anything he does is not his fault.

I know that the breakdown of the family in this country has set so many of our youth adrift without the discipline or guidance they so desperately need, but passive acquiescence to their petty crimes will most certainly lead them to believe that they can get away with anything in this permissive, silly society of ours. It's downright injustice to the young people of today to allow them to think that they can go through life without any authority, which is the reason so many of them end up in a prison cell or dead in some filthy alley.

Of course I understand that graffiti is just the tip of an iceberg which would terrify us if we could see what was actually under the water, but I think that a zero tolerance policy for graffiti would at least be a start. A way of saying to these young people, "You belong to a society that will not tolerate your insolence; we will not have our buildings defaced, our monuments defiled nor our public transportation a billboard for your personal rebellion. You will be held accountable for your acts. You will undo what you've done, you will personally right the wrong, and you will satisfy your debt."

TO PROTECT AND SERVE

Recently in Nashville there was a bank robbery that ended with the bank robber running into the woods behind the bank and engaging in a pitched gun battle with the police. It ended in his death, the slight wounding of two officers, and the death of one police dog who took a bullet for his handler.

The TV crews arrived on the scene very early in the incident and got the biggest part of the action on live TV. Though you couldn't actually see the fugitive you could hear the gunshots and see the officers firing into the woods.

It really brought home to me just how vital a good police force is. These are the men and women who put themselves in harm's way every day. They are our last line of defense and all that separates us from the jungle.

It takes a dedicated and brave person to be a police officer. They stand against tremendous odds. Not only do they battle crime but they have to deal with a clogged and often benign court system which seems to take great delight in returning criminals to the streets.

They are faced with so many technicalities that it's a wonder they're ever able to make a charge stick, such is our courts' preoccupation with the rights of the criminals.

And in too many instances they find themselves in an adversary's role with a press corps who are more concerned with political correctness than with justice.

It's got to be hard being a cop these days. Every time a police officer stops a car for a routine traffic violation, he or she never knows when the driver is going to pull out a gun and start blasting. It takes constant vigilance just to stay alive.

Every year there are men and women who are killed in the line of duty. People with families, people who had a life to live, a life cut short protecting you and me.

It seems that our press, in many cases, are more concerned with ridiculing our peace officers than in letting the public know the good things they do every day.

I certainly do not defend the officers who beat Rodney King; in fact, it was a deplorable thing. But did anybody ever stop to think that if Rodney King had not been breaking the law and endangering the lives of other citizens with his driving, he would never have been stopped by the police to begin with?

I wonder what the press would have said had Rodney King plowed into a crowded bus stop or into the playground of a day-care center. Would the LAPD have been blamed for not stopping his rampage? I think so.

And I wonder what the press would have said about the federal agencies involved had they left well enough alone and the Branch Davidians had sallied forth and turned their considerable firepower on the good people of Waco.

If you don't like the police, the next time you're in danger call a lawyer.

TOTAL DISGUST

From this day forward I don't want anybody to defend the feminist movement to me because I am so totally disgusted with Gloria Steinem, Anita Hill, and all the rest of the loudmouthed charlatans who run around claiming to represent the women of this country that I could literally throw up.

What a bunch of hypocrites. According to them, Clarence Thomas should not be allowed to serve on the Supreme Court because he "allegedly" made a couple of off-color remarks to Anita Hill, but it's all right for Bill Clinton to put his hands all over a woman—to expose himself to her—and it's OK because he's the darling of the feminist movement.

Wake up, America; these people are evil. Do you really believe that these ladies, and I use the term lightly, really care about all the women in this country? No, they're only interested in helping the women who ascribe to their political agenda, and don't you ever think any different. They're not only evil, they're dangerous, elitist, and downright bigots.

Now before you start calling me all the nasty little names that the feminists reserve for males who disagree with them, let me tell you that women run my company, and my life, for that matter. They are department heads and are some of the most valued and important employees that I have.

They're the best, and they command the utmost respect from fellow employees and the business people they deal with. If somebody who worked for me put a hand on any of them in the manner that Bill Clinton put his hand on those women, I would not only immediately fire that person but I would probably lose my temper and try to separate his head from his body.

We also have a lady truck driver who does a bang-up job, and the same goes for her. She is treated with the greatest respect.

I would also vote for a woman for president. I think it's time that we gave them a shot at it. It seems that the men aren't doing too well at it.

But I will never vote for one of these hypocritical feminists who abandon their sisters to side with the likes of Bill Clinton, who has a long and sordid history of sexual harassment. Yes, abandon them to be kicked around by slime balls like James Carville, who try to destroy their reputations and make it look as if all that happened to them was their fault.

Well, let me tell you how I feel about it. I don't care about the reputations of the women who accused Bill Clinton. It doesn't make any difference if they are street walkers or Sunday school teachers. Whatever they are it doesn't give Bill Clinton the right to put his grubby hands on them.

STILL IN CHARGE

The other night I was watching TV, one of the plethora of specials on the Clinton debacle.

As I listened to the sordid details of his sleazy affair with Monica Lewinsky, and even more distressing, listened to people saying that what he did was a private matter and should not have been brought up for public scrutiny, I became more and more depressed.

It was very evident that the morality of this country had failed to an all time low as person after person said something to the effect that, the country's doing pretty good so we should just leave Bill Clinton alone and let him continue to be president.

Admittedly, there were also people calling for his resignation and impeachment. But a good portion of this country is willing to have a president who is a proven liar just because the economy is pretty good (an economy that he had very little to do with creating, as far as I'm concerned).

This president tries to hide behind a Robin Hood-type facade of taking from the rich and giving to the poor, of being the champion of the downtrodden, the savior of Social Security and the bane of the evil tobacco companies, when all the while he is taking advantage of an empty headed, power-smitten, foolish young woman.

Jim Baker and Jimmy Swaggart were held up for public ridicule for less lurid affairs than what the president had. Nobody defended them.

The entire military community is held to a rigid standard of conduct when it comes to sex—a different standard than their commander in chief, evidently.

As I watched all this trash I realized how deeply worried I was about the future of America. It just seemed that things would never be completely all right ever again.

For some reason or another, I flipped the channel during the commercial and there was Billy Graham proclaiming the eternal good news about Jesus Christ, and there it was, the truth of truths, almighty God is still in charge.

No matter how impossible things seem, He's still there, He knows, and He cares. He will set it all straight one of these days.

The most important thing that we can do is to receive the salvation that He gave us through His son Jesus, and then no matter what happens we're ready for anything.

We should never put our trust in mere man. They're going to mess up like President Clinton. We should put our trust in God who never messes up.

LEGACY

A lot has been said about President Clinton's legacy, how he will be perceived by future generations, how he will be remembered and portrayed by historians.

I'm sure that when he came into office his expectations were stratospheric. Would he be remembered for some high ideal social revolution that would put food in the mouths of the hungry, better educate an intellectually waning America, make medical care accessible to all, abolish ghettos, elevate minorities, and break once and for all the glass ceiling of male dominance in the workplace?

Would he at last put some teeth into the war on drugs, get tough with the dealers and the kingpins who prey on the most vulnerable of our population?

Or, perhaps, would he be remembered for some foreign policy coup? At long last putting Saddam in his place or telling the Chinese that as long as they have such an atrocious human rights record that they will not be a most favored trading nation?

Would he make our streets safer, our military stronger, our future more secure?

Would he be the kind of leader who would encourage morality, a role model for great and small to aspire to?

I think we all know the answer to those questions. Bill Clinton will most likely be remembered as the man who, much like

Esau, sold his birthright for a bowl of soup, only in his case he sold ours for even less noble reasons.

Of course the United States of America is much bigger than one president, so as long as the economy is good Bill Clinton's legacy shouldn't matter so much. Right?

Wrong!!! The problem is that Bill Clinton's legacy is going to be our legacy, the things that he has done in office will affect this nation for generations to come and very possibly until the end of our history.

The only thing this president has going for him is a good economy that he had very little to do with. In fact, left to his own devices, he would have ruined the economy totally in his very first term with Hillary's potentially catastrophic attempt to take over medical care. A thinly veiled piece of pure socialism, such as seems to be so dear to this president's heart.

He claims to "feel our pain," to really care about everybody, race, color or creed notwithstanding, and yet he has done more to drive a stake between the races in this nation than any president since Reconstruction, by insinuating that the minorities' troubles are caused by a non-caring Republican Congress that wants to starve children and kick senior citizens out in the cold, and a callous white populous with an attitude just to the right of one of Bull Connor's German police dogs.

He portrays himself as the modern day John Brown, but his Trojan horse tactics will backfire. And America will pay the price. Clinton's legacy.

Nobody really knows the extent of Clinton's sellout to the Communist Chinese, but the day may well come when we are threatened with our own technology. Clinton's legacy.

Our Congress is locked in mortal combat, the Democrats trying to defend a morally bankrupt political party with semantics, spin, and downright dishonesty. The Democrats and Republicans are at each other's throats worse than ever. Clinton's legacy.

When can you ever believe another word that a president says? Clinton's legacy.

What do you tell your six-year-old when she asks you what oral sex is? Clinton's legacy.

When we need our military and find that they've been gutted and demoralized, what do we do? Don't ask; don't tell? Clinton's legacy.

When Saddam Hussein starts raining down chemical and nuclear weapons on his neighbors and we stand on the brink of the Third World War and the United Nations is recognized as the powerless, socialistic paper tiger that it's always been, who will we turn to? Clinton's legacy.

Bill Clinton will most likely be long gone when the ramifications of his actions come full circle, but I've got a feeling that the America we've known is gone forever.

We will be a less trusting, less demanding, less moral nation with two sets of laws, one for the masses and one for the powerful. It won't really matter what you do as long as you can get away with it.

The women's movement has taken a giant step backwards, forsaken by its more militant sisters who have their own political agenda having little to do with real women's rights.

After all these years of work and struggle, has the image of the working woman been reduced to a pawn of the powerful? An object to be used and discarded like a piece of Kleenex in a wastebasket in the Oval Office? Clinton's legacy.

PART 2
WHY I LOVE AMERICA

We're walking
real proud
and we're talking
real loud again.

—*"In America,"*
from ***Full Moon*****, *1980***

MY BEAUTIFUL AMERICA

Have you ever spent the late afternoon watching the purple shadows deepen in the Arizona desert, or seen a herd of elk plow their way through waist deep snow on a cold Colorado dawn?

Did you ever watch the sun go down in Hawaii or see the stormy waves break over the rock-bound coast of Maine, or have you ever seen an eagle fly up out of the mists of Alaska or a big October moon hanging full over the still Dakota Bad Lands?

Have you ever tasted the gumbo in New Orleans, the barbecue in Carolina, or the chicken wings in Buffalo? Have you ever had Brunswick stew in Macon or cornbread in Birmingham or brisket slow-cooked over hill country mesquite wood?

Did you ever drink water from a gurgling branch in Utah or stand on the mountain above El Paso del Norte and see the lights twinkling clear over into Mexico?

Did you ever jingle horses in the predawn stillness of a perfect Texas day and watch their shod hooves kicking up sparks on the volcanic rock, or tended a trot line on a foggy Carolina morning, or heard the distant song of a lovesick whippoorwill in the pristine Tennessee late night?

Have you seen the faces on Mount Rushmore or stood at the Vietnam monument? Have you ever crossed the mighty Mississippi or been to the Daddy of 'Em All in Cheyenne, Wyoming, or seen the mighty Vols run out on the football field on a chilly autumn afternoon?

Did you ever see the Chicago skyline from Lakeshore Drive at night or the New England foliage in the fall or the summer beauty of the Shenandoah Valley or Indiana covered with new snow?

Did you ever see a herd of wild horses running free across the empty spaces of Nevada or caught a walleye pike out of a cold Wisconsin stream, or marveled at the tall ships docked in the harbor at Baltimore?

Did you ever see the early morning dew sparkling on the bluegrass or the wind stir the wheat fields on a hot Kansas afternoon or driven the lonely stretches of old Route 66?

Have you ever heard the church bells peal their call to worship on an early Sunday in some small town in the Deep South, or passed through the redwood forests as the sun was going down?

Have you ever been to Boise or Baxley or Beaufort or Billings? Have you ever passed through Sanford or Suffolk or San Angelo? Have you seen the falls at Niagara, the Ice Palace in St. Paul, or the Gateway to the West?

This then is America, the land God blesses with everything, and no Eiffel Tower, no Taj Mahal, no Alps, nor Andes, no native hut, nor royal palace can rival her awesome beauty, her diverse population, her monolithic majesty. America the free, America the mighty, America the beautiful.

ALASKA: AN IMPRESSION

We've just returned from a short concert tour of Alaska, and I've just got to say, folks, it's one of the most beautiful, the most interesting, and the most fascinating places that I've ever had the privilege of visiting.

This was my third time to our forty-ninth state, but it was the first time that I've been able to view the landscape from ground level, and I'll tell you, friends, it's breathtaking.

On a bus ride down the Kenai Peninsula we saw mountain sheep, a moose, and I couldn't tell how many bald eagles. There was even one perched on a lamp pole beside the highway.

Alaska is truly a sportsman's dream. People up there literally have to chase moose out of their yards and they talk about fifty-pound salmon as if they were as common as catfish. They have just about every kind of animal that lives on the North American continent and quite a few never seen in the lower forty-eight.

They have black bear, brown bear, grizzly bear, Kodiak bear, polar bear, moose, caribou, reindeer, mule deer, badgers, foxes, wolverines, rabbits, squirrels and wolves.

They have beautiful mountains, pristine forests, clean streams, the northern lights and wonderful, friendly people.

The food in Alaska is fantastic. The folks up there can do things to seafood that can make your tongue slap your eyeballs out, and when was the last time you had reindeer sausage for breakfast?

Alaska is not all boondocks, either. Anchorage is a striving, bustling city of 250,000 complete with tall buildings and traffic jams.

You have to admire the good people of Alaska. They're a hardy breed who have a "cut to the chase, let's get the job done" attitude, who keep their own counsel and do things their own way.

Years ago when the Alaskan pipeline was proposed, there were dire warnings from ecology groups that it would destroy the tundra and the wildlife there. Well, Alaska went on and did it anyway, and they turned out to be right. The caribou herd has actually increased since the advent of the pipeline.

When the Valdez oil spill happened, they didn't sit around moaning about it. They rolled up their sleeves and cleaned the mess up.

I believe that they have proven that man can live in harmony with nature and still enjoy hunting, fishing, and harvesting timber.

Alaska was purchased from the Russians at about the time the Civil War was winding down and received its statehood in 1959. It is our largest state in land mass and one of our smallest population-wise.

The people of Alaska are rightfully proud of their wonderful state, and I don't blame them. I'm kinda proud of it myself.

THE BEAUTIFUL ROCKY MOUNTAINS

Among the many beautiful sights that God created, few hold more fascination and allure for me than the Rocky Mountains.

I had been through the Rockies many times and certainly appreciated their beauty, but my appreciation was superficial compared to the love I have developed for the them since having the opportunity to spend some time there.

Rugged, majestic, and snowcapped, they tower above our little valley splashed with aspens, and sprinkled with pines with a miniature river babbling its boulder-strewn way along the bottom of the canyon.

Grand home of elk, bear, and eagle, and summertime playground for the myriad hummingbirds who gather the nectar from the multicolored carpet of wildflowers which cover the mountainside like a patchwork quilt.

Sometimes the sky gets so blue that it almost doesn't seem real and at night the stars hang low in the unpolluted sky and the moon is so bright you could almost read by it.

When the big storms come and the north wind comes roaring down the canyon blowing the big flakes this way and that, sometimes it leaves two feet of snow behind, giving us a white world, pristine and virgin.

The icicles hang off the eaves of the house growing longer by the day.

The evergreens gather snow and the boughs hang down under the weight, until the wind comes whistling down the canyon and they sway and shudder and shed their white blankets and stand tall and proud again.

The citizens are a tough and hardy people, friendly and helpful, who respect your privacy and expect you to respect theirs.

There are many beautiful towns in the Rocky Mountains but my very favorite is Durango. Quaint and quality, busy and easygoing, with its architecture frozen in the 1800s, and its attitude as modern as tomorrow's newspaper. A mile-high village in the sky with a rich past and a richer future, nestled in the breathtaking high country called the Four Corners.

When the spring warms up and the snowpack begins to melt, the Animas and La Plata swell and rush along bearing kayaks and rafts and all manner of fun and folks.

Will it always be this way? Will there always be a pristine view, an unpolluted starry night, and acres of virgin snow that has known neither tire track nor footprint?

Or will the greedy hand of progress reach out and strangle the fragile way of life, scattering condominiums and crime, sidewalks and superhighways, grit and grime and graft?

I hope not, I pray not. I hope that future generations can step out of the world, as I did, and find the peace, the serenity, and the astounding beauty of the Rocky Mountains.

COLORADO

I woke up early one morning and got out of bed a little after four o'clock. We had a big wet snow overnight and the scrub oak forests looked like a giant cotton patch in the silver of the moonlight.

Looking across the La Plata Canyon with all that snow clinging to the trees is one of the most beautiful sights you could ever hope to see: Colorado at its best.

The Four Corners area is such a special place, unhurried, friendly, and breathtakingly beautiful. If you're into history, sightseeing or just plain fun, you just can't beat it. From the ancient cliff dwellings at Mesa Verde to the brand new Southwest Center for the Arts. In Durango there's something for everybody. Skiing, dog sledding, snow boarding, and sleigh rides help make up the myriad activities available and there's a little steam train which makes a daily round trip through some rocky mountain country that will have your eyes popping.

Durango boasts some of the finest restaurants you'll find anyplace on Planet Earth. Francisco's serves *muy bueno* Mexican food, Chez Grande Mere is the best French restaurant I've ever set foot in, and Ariano's serves great northern Italian food—just to name a few—but just about any place that hangs out a shingle is a pretty safe bet in Durango.

Hazel and I found a new passion on our winter vacation this year when we discovered snowmobiling. Flying across the snow, up and down hills, and scooting through the wooded trails on a snowmobile is just too much fun.

And wildlife: I've seen elk, bald eagles and one day a coyote came right up on our patio.

We've made friends in Colorado, good folks who will go out of their way to help you out. Everybody minds his own business and lets you mind your own.

There's a performing arts hall in Durango which does over fifty events a year, ranging from a Russian Balalaika Band to the Four Corners Symphony Orchestra.

There is no other experience I've had quite like watching a couple of feet of fluffy snow fall as a big storm works its way down the La Plata Canyon, when the world turns white and you can't even see the mountains across the way.

And walking into a cold clear Colorado night is another reminder of what a beautiful universe God made. There are so many stars and they're so bright. You can pick out the constellations one by one and the moon can be so bright that you could almost read a book by it.

If this sounds like a commercial for Colorado I don't mean it to. We've just returned from there and I wanted to write down some of my thoughts while they're still fresh in my mind.

It's just a great place, pristine and unspoiled, and a wonderful place to spend time.

Ain't America wonderful?

CROSS-COUNTRY BACK ROADS

Hazel and I recently drove from Durango, Colorado, to Nashville and decided to shun the interstate and take the back roads for the first part of the trip.

The first hundred miles brought us to Wolf Creek Pass, Colorado, a place so beautiful that I have trouble even finding words to describe it. The mountains, the sheer rock cliffs, and the stately lodge pole pines blend together in a landscape that can almost take your breath away.

It's hard to decide which way to look when straight ahead is a magnificent mountain, to the right a drop-off to a creek several hundred feet below, and to the left a faraway valley that appears to go on forever, and the deep snow and the frozen streams are just the icing on the cake.

We spent the night in Raton, New Mexico, and got up before the sun did the next morning and headed east through the New Mexican back country where you can drive for fifty miles and never even meet another car.

The sun was just painting the mountains a dusty rose color when we rounded a curve and a herd of elk were jumping the fence about fifty yards in front of us on the right. Off to the left in the distance we saw another herd of elk, the big bulls with their massive racks held high at a prideful angle looking back across the meadow at us, the intruders.

A little farther along was a herd of elk, a couple of coyotes, and at least a hundred turkeys. I still haven't figured out whether they were wild or domestic.

We took Route 451 across a huge plateau, cattle country, summer pasture with no cattle this time of year but miles and miles of barbed wire, working pens, corrals, and empty camps where the cowboys would spread their bedrolls in the spring when the cattle were brought back to the high country.

Black rock, red clay, and blue sky mile after mile. Serenity, no traffic, a feast for the eyes and a joy for the soul. God's handiwork. The wide open spaces at their best. Stretching from horizon to horizon, rising, falling, the colors changing as the sun climbed higher in a perfect sky, a Gary Morton painting come to life.

Hazel was driving and I said, "Well, we've got plenty of gas, let's just go on and the worst thing that could happen would be that we'd have to stop and turn around."

Twenty-five miles later we hit paved road again and wound our way up to the Black Mesa area, the highest point in Oklahoma. And then we were zipping along the panhandle with Kansas a few miles to the north and Texas a few miles to the south.

And then it was irrigation systems, radio towers, and traffic, and all too soon we were on four lanes of civilization and back in the real world.

Oh, I know that the great Western Outback is not never-never land. I know that somewhere out there there's a satellite dish with CNN spouting off about the stock market and the sex lives of careless politicians.

And I know they have car payments, and income tax, and a thousand other things which complicate their lives.

I realize that they are not insulated from a nosy, greedy, government or the price of gasoline.

But when they get up in the morning they're not face to face with pollution. They can go to bed without worrying about somebody breaking in during the night and they can ride a horse from hell to breakfast without ever having to open a single gate.

Toy Caldwell wrote a song called "Take the Highway," but knowing Toy as I did, I'd say that given the choice he would have taken the back roads.

NEW YORK

Of all the places I've ever been to in my life, I've never found any place quite like New York City. To a country boy it's mystical and intimidating, loud and rowdy. A hustling, bustling beehive where everybody's trying to get somewhere in a hurry and determined to get there no matter how many people they have to go around or over the top of.

New York is a city of contradictions and shadow. You can walk down the street and see the latest fashion and the outrageous intentionally out-of-fashion, lavish opulence and abject poverty, authenticity, eccentricity, super-shyness, and outlandish exhibitionism, all within a few blocks of each other.

It seems that New Yorkers are always in a hurry, but they will always take the time to tell you where Saks Fifth Avenue is or how to get to the Empire State Building.

You can hear every language known to mankind on the streets of New York, and whatever New Yorkers undertake they're going to do it bigger and better than anybody else. They have the tallest buildings, the loudest boom boxes, the most taxi cabs, and the busiest airports of any place I know.

If you can't get it in New York City it very likely doesn't exist. They have every kind of food, every style of clothes, every make of car, every shade of lipstick etc., etc.

You never run out of things to do in New York—why, just walking down the street is entertainment. There's no telling what you might see, anything from a movie star to a tourist from Joplin with two cameras and a guidebook gawking up at the tall buildings in Midwestern innocence and snapping pictures right and left to show to the folks back home.

I guess New York tops the list of most folks' "nice place to visit, wouldn't want to live there" places. And yet you get the impression that most of the people who live there wouldn't even think about living someplace else.

If you've never been to New York City I would advise you to go at least one time. But then you'll probably be like me: One time will never be enough.

I think New York's a trip.

TAKING UP FOR BOBBY

I recently read a book titled *Down the Highway: The Life of Bob Dylan*, by a guy named Howard Sounes. It was an unauthorized biography of Bob Dylan. Mr. Sounes interviewed me for the book, since I had had the honor of being a small part of three Bob Dylan albums. I played on *Nashville Skyline, Self Portrait*, and *New Morning*.

By the conversation I had with him, I assumed that it would be an informative, upbeat book celebrating the life and music of one of the greatest musical poets the world has ever known.

Wrong. Mr. Sounes attempted a hatchet job on Bob Dylan much in the fashion that Albert Goldman did on Elvis Presley.

He painted a picture of a vindictive, hard-nosed, individual who took advantage of situations and was unfaithful to his friends. He seemed to take delight in belittling Dylan's numerous and incredible accomplishments and emphasizing his problems and failures.

The part that really got me was his total misunderstanding of Bob Dylan's conversion to Christianity. He wrote about it as if it were an albatross around his neck insofar as his career was concerned. He berated Bob for talking about God on stage, and just couldn't understand that Bob Dylan had gone through a life-changing experience and wanted to share it with the world.

He painted a totally different picture from the one I have always had of Bob Dylan after spending admittedly a limited amount of time with him. But I just can't believe that I'm that bad a judge of character.

The Bob Dylan I remember was fun to work with and fun to be around. With a sense of humor and friendly and courteous manner toward the people with whom he was working, he had a way of making you feel free to do your own thing when you were in the studio with him.

Dylan didn't use the cookie cutter method of recording over and over again, overdubbing, composite vocals, and absolute perfection. He was into getting the point across, letting the instruments surround his poetry, pushing it to the top and making those magnificent phrases he wrote stick out and tease the senses of those of us who, in many cases, were trying to figure out just what he meant by this line or that.

Bob never belabored the point. If the first take suited his fancy, that was the one that was used, imperfections be damned. And who can argue with a man who has sold over fifty million records, totally changed the face of popular music, and inspired a generation of young artists and songwriters?

Bob values his privacy probably more than most people because he's had a hard time having very much of if for the last forty years. He may be a little eccentric, but who isn't in their own way. And different? Of course he's different. If he wasn't he wouldn't be the unique person that he is. But that doesn't mean that he is not an ordinary human being in a lot of other ways.

I remember him as the family man who brought his wife, Sara, and his young son, Jesse, to Nashville when he recorded *Nashville Skyline*. I remember him as the giant who gave a bottom-of-the-totem-pole guitar player a chance to be a part of musical history. There's only one Bob Dylan, and I'm thankful to have had the opportunity to walk in his shadow for a season.

A NICE LITTLE GUY

This past week the music community lost a talented, pace-setting member when George Harrison died from cancer in Los Angeles.

Of course, George is best known for being one of the Beatles, but I sometimes wonder if the world really realizes what an important part of that super-successful group he really was. Quiet and soft-spoken, and most often eclipsed by the phenomenal success of Lennon and McCartney, he stood on stage and played his guitar, sang harmony, and wrote his songs.

A little less flamboyant than the other three, but with a tenderness and vulnerability that endeared him to so many around the world.

But George's contribution to the Beatles' legend was to become apparent to the whole planet with his composition of "Something," in my opinion one of the greatest of the Beatles' songs.

George had a way with melodies and chords that was quite unique, a tenderness of lyric and a very personal vocal delivery. His influence on the group is evident in their early work with George's rockabilly guitar style. He was a big Carl Perkins fan and it really came out in those early days.

I met George in New York on a happenstance. I just happened to be in town, and George and Bob Dylan wanted to spend some time in the studio together, and Dylan's producer, Bob Johnston, called and asked if I'd like to come down to the studio and play bass with them. Well, of course I did, and along with a drummer named Russ Kunkle we spent the biggest part of the afternoon just jamming and playing old and new Dylan songs and whatever else they decided to do. It was a great day in my life, not just because of working with one of the Beatles and Bob Dylan, but because the atmosphere was one of four guys, just having fun in a recording studio.

It was shortly after Paul left the group, and George laughingly asked me, "Do you want to be a Beatle?" He was such a gentleman, congenial and conversational, just one of the boys with an English accent. Needless to say, I thoroughly enjoyed the day.

I never saw George again until twenty-some years later at a restaurant in Los Angeles where he was having dinner with some friends. I stopped by the table and paid my respects and was treated with the same warmth and friendliness as the last time I had seen him years before in New York.

George truly cared for his fellow man and proved it by organizing the concert for Bangladesh and then fighting it out with Capitol Records to have the *Resultant* album released.

It's hard to realize that it's been nearly forty years since those mop tops from Liverpool set the entertainment world on its ear with their music and mystique—so many classic songs that it boggles the mind to try and remember them all.

The Beatles as individuals were incredibly talented but as a group the combination of their talents was truly astounding.

The right combination of people, the right mix of musical tastes and attitudes and temperaments to turn out music that will transcend their lifetimes by many years. A truly classic body of work and none was more classic nor classy than the thin, young man from Liverpool, George Harrison.

ELVIS

To say that Elvis was one of my heroes would be like calling the Pacific Ocean a mud puddle. In the early days I hung on every word that he sang, every wiggle of his celebrated hips, every record, every movie, every Elvis thing that came along.

Elvis generated excitement like no one ever has before or since. He was a genuine, bona fide, megasuperstar, the first of that breed. We just couldn't get enough of him.

The Beatles, Michael Jackson, and their ilk have kicked up some excitement in their day too but nothing like The Pelvis. There was a mystique about him; nobody could ever quite figure out what he was.

I guess he was a lot of things: a southern-fried honky tonker, a hymn-singing hell raiser, a down-home mama's boy who lived the Cinderella story to the hilt. Who but Elvis ever had the gall to buy seven Cadillacs at one time?

He did the things that we dared not even dream about except in our wildest and most private fantasies. He gave away fortunes in jewels and cars, he dated movie stars, he wore hip clothes, he defied society, but not in any rebel sort of way. I think Elvis just wanted to be himself.

He was the cock of the walk, the toast of the town, the cat's pajamas, the crème de la crème, the boy from the projects who could thumb his nose at all the people from the right side of the tracks.

He made shallow, cookie-cutter movies with watered-down plots and terrible songs, but we didn't care, we went to see them anyway. As long as his name was on the marquee that was good enough.

The pity of that situation is that a lot of people, myself included, think that Elvis could have been a real actor, given the chance, but we'll never know for sure, will we?

He went to the army and the whole world waited with bated breath to see what he was going to do when he finally came back to us. We got our answer soon enough; he just took up where he left off, and we all found out that we'd been saving a place in our hearts for him anyway.

We owe a lot to Elvis. I know I do. He had a profound influence on me, but not just his contemporaries. Kids who weren't even alive when Elvis died owe him a debt of gratitude, because he started it all.

Every time some kid cranks his amplifier up on ten and puts his Stratocaster through the paces, there's a little bit of Elvis there. When the house lights fall and a lightning bolt of excitement streaks through the crowd there's a little bit of Elvis there.

America had a love affair with Elvis Aaron Presley that lasted for over a quarter of a century. We saw him at his best and we saw him at his worst. He made us laugh, he made us cry, and at times maybe even scared us a little bit.

Even after being gone for over twenty years, his records still sell, his memory is honored and cherished, and Elvis impersonators are as common as dishrags.

He was a true phenomenon, partly truth, partly legend, the Pied Piper in blue suede shoes, the cat, the king, the one and only Elvis.

REMEMBERING

It is approaching the anniversary of the horrible Lynyrd Skynyrd tragedy. Twenty-five years since October 20, 1977—that sad night when we lost our friends in a plane crash.

I still think about Ronnie and find myself talking about him. He was a friend that I'm so glad I got to know, and I treasure the hours that we spent together. I miss him.

I miss Toy and Tommy Caldwell. We spent so much time touring together. The Marshall Tucker Band and the CDB crisscrossed this country playing our concerts night after night and developed a friendship that exists to this day with some of the surviving members of the band.

You've got to admire Gary Rossington and Billy Powell. They have withstood more heartache and lost more friends than anybody I know in the music business. First Ronnie Van Zant, Steve and Cassie Gaines, along with roadie Dean Kilpatrick in the '77 plane crash. Then a few years later, Allen Collins passed away, and more recently, Leon Wilkerson.

But the guys keep on going and for that I admire you, my brothers.

And you've got to hand it to Doug Gray. After the catastrophic loss of Toy and Tommy Caldwell he continues to tour the country putting out that great Marshall Tucker sound.

I have a special place in my heart for these two bands and was deeply hurt by the losses they suffered. Road bands, I guess, are a different breed, and only they can truly understand each other. The call of the never-ending highway, the glare of the spotlight, the applause of the crowds. The satisfaction of entertaining people with something you have created yourself all go together to form an addiction which we all share in common.

And it takes a powerful addiction to keep a man away from home and hearth two hundred nights a year. Cramped motel rooms, truck stop food, and thousands of miles bouncing down the road on a bus can't dull the desire.

There are a few people who pass through your life that become so special that you can remember the place and the circumstances when you heard about their dying.

I was in St. Louis in a hotel room when I got the news that Ronnie Van Zant had been killed in the plane crash.

I was in a hotel room in California when I found out about Tommy Caldwell.

Oddly enough we were playing Radio City Music Hall with Lynyrd Skynyrd the day that I found out about Toy Caldwell.

These people were special to me, and though they are not with us anymore, they will occupy a space in my heart.

So much of them lives on in the great music they left behind. When we hear "Freebird" or "Can't You See" or "Sweet Home Alabama" or "Take the Highway" we are reminded that there were some people who passed through this world who left a legacy of music which will live on and on. Enriching the lives of generations to come.

God bless the survivors and the families of the Lynyrd Skynyrd band and the Marshall Tucker Band.

Remember, Charlie loves you, everyone.

THE GRAND OLE OPRY

It's Saturday and in a few hours the band and I will be mounting the stage at the Grand Ole Opry. It is an honor and a dream that I thought was almost impossible when I was a young fiddle player listening to the Opry and trying to imagine what it would be like to actually see it.

I remember the first time I ever attended the Opry. It was in 1955 or so, and a bunch of my buddies and I made what was then the long, long trip to Nashville, Tennessee. Stood in line for tickets and stayed until the last note was played. Then we went around the corner to the Midnite Jamboree at the Ernest Tubb Record Shop and then drove back to Carolina, tired but happy.

I remember the first time I actually played the Opry as a member of the Earl Scruggs Revue. Walking on that stage was an awesome experience. It was at the old Ryman Auditorium and there were so many stars backstage that it could make your head spin. Roy Acuff, Bill Monroe, Porter Wagoner, and Dolly Parton, legends in the flesh.

And then the first time I ever took the stage with the Charlie Daniels Band. It is a real privilege to walk on that stage and go out over WSM 650, the radio station that has been synonymous with country for over seventy-five years. Bill Cody, a DJ friend of mine, calls it "The Mother Church" of country music.

There was a time when you weren't considered at the top of the country music business if you didn't appear on the Grand Ole Opry. Hank Williams, Ernest Tubb, Eddie Arnold, Ray Price, Little Jimmie Dickens, and countless other stars in the country music constellation were Grand Ole Opry regulars.

It's like no other show in the world and has been broadcast continuously every Saturday night except for one for over seventy-five years.

The Opry has attracted audiences from around the world and has maintained its "countryness" through change and challenge, trend and fad. You can get back to your roots at the Opry. I spent countless hours in Roy Acuff's dressing room listening to stories about how it used to be when Roy Acuff and the Smoky Mountain Boys did concerts in places that didn't even have electricity.

It seemed there was always a jam session going on in Bill Monroe's dressing room, and the bluegrass music resonating out of that door was the best in the world.

Cousin Minnie Pearl always had a smile and that hat with the price tag hanging off the side, a sweet and talented lady who is as much a part of the Opry tradition as the old-time fiddle tunes the square dancers clog to every Saturday night.

I will walk on that stage tonight and savor every second. It's an experience I'll always value and never forget. Something no one can take away from us.

Tonight when the band takes the stage, it won't be just any of the stages we mount over a hundred times a year. It will be a special and exciting feeling, exhilarating and yet humbling, like walking onto the pages of a history book where so many of my heroes have walked before.

The Grand Ole Opry, the rootinest, tootinest country music the world has ever known. Long live the Opry!!!!!

MUSIC

So you want to make it in the music business? I've been asked about this subject so much that I've decided to devote this column to trying to answer some of the questions.

First and foremost, never deceive yourself about the amount of talent that you have.

Secondly, make very sure that you really want a career in the music business, because it's not easy and if you don't have the desire and tenacity to stick it out there's no need in starting out.

Thirdly, if you want to be in the music business you have to be somewhere where there is a music business to be in. You can't sit in some place a thousand miles away from the action and expect to make any headway.

And here's the part that most people don't want to hear. You have to go at it full-time. Music is a very jealous and demanding profession. So you have to give up your daytime job and go for it.

If you agree with what I've written so far, now we can get down to business.

First of all, are you a songwriter, a singer, a guitar picker, or someone who wants to work behind the scenes?

You need to set some goals.

My first goal was just to make a living playing music.

Then I wanted to play in better places.

Then I wanted to make a record, then a gold record, then a platinum record, and so on.

So, if you're like me, as you attain one goal, you'll set another one a little bit higher.

Never measure yourself by someone else.

When I first started out some of my contemporaries had hit records right away and I had to make five albums before we really got anything significant going.

Are you willing to work when everybody else is playing? Are you willing to be the first one to get there and the last one to leave? Can you stand being openly criticized by some arrogant person that doesn't have as much talent in his whole body as you have in your little finger?

Can you smile when you feel like crying, can you persevere when you're tired or sick or worried? Are you willing to work twice as hard as everybody else if that's what it takes?

Can you walk on stage without taking your personal problems with you?

Can you manage to get up one more time than you get knocked down?

Success is pyramid-shaped. There's plenty of room at the bottom, but the closer you get to the pinnacle the less room there is until, at the very top, there's room for only one.

How high do you want to climb?

Music is a demanding taskmaster. It requires your best, your unremitting commitment, your absolute belief that there is indeed gold at the end of the rainbow.

There is no magic wand, no yellow brick roads, no shortcuts.

There's only talent, tenacity, sweat, and faith, and the deep conviction that you've got something that people are willing to pay money to see and hear, something unique to you, that nobody else does quite the way you do.

Sound tough? It is.

Welcome to the music business.

LETTER FROM A SOLDIER

I'm going to do something different this week in this column. I'm going to publish a letter that I got from a soldier while we were touring the military bases in Korea.

I am not doing this because of the wonderful things she had to say about me, but because I believe that she has defined the reason we went to Korea to begin with, and so succinctly describes the patriotism of the young people who proudly wear the uniform of the United States of America.

"To the Charlie Daniels Band:

"I wanted to take a moment and thank you for what you're doing in South Korea. I am sure you have received many thanks from the soldiers you have entertained and those you have had the opportunity to speak to. This is a simple note that you can read in the quiet moments from a soldier that was proud to be reminded that America has not forgotten us.

"In the era of an all-volunteer army where there were conflicts, not wars; there were quiet deployments and not well-documented battles; and the fighting was in some remote location nowhere near threatening our own borders, the soldier was forgotten. The recent tragedies have opened the eyes of many to a truth that many of us have known all along, the world is full of heroes. I see them every day, I work with them every day. The parade grounds and gymnasiums you have played were filled with them. Everyone you have

taken the time to shake hands with, to sign an autograph for, or just to say thanks to has appreciated it. Your dedication to the troops makes you heroes also. You stand in the spotlight, in a position to reach and influence many and support America, support pride and support the military. For that you have my deepest and most sincere appreciation.

"I love my job. Flying is my passion. I could have flown in the civilian world, but like many of the faces you've looked into this week I wanted something more. I wanted to serve my country. We all raised our right hands and swore to lay our lives down to protect the freedom of those we love, those we know, and even those who protest against what we do. Standing outside the aircraft at Camp Casey, in my flight gear saluting the flag, I was once again reminded of why I joined the army. Every time I stand at attention and salute the flag tears still fill my eyes, chills run down my spine, and my heart swells with pride to be a member of the armed forces. Your visit here, your obvious pride in what we do has made a difference in a difficult deployment in South Korea for many soldiers. I was proud to have the opportunity to fly you around the South Korean peninsula, proud to be a part of what you've done here. These simple words cannot begin to convey the extent of my gratitude, but they will have to do.

"Thank you,

"CW2 Beth McCune"

It is the soldier, not the reporter, who has given us freedom of the press.

It is the soldier, not the poet, who has given us freedom of speech.

It is the soldier, not the campus organizer, who has given us freedom to demonstrate.

It is the soldier who salutes the flag, who serves beneath the flag and whose coffin is draped by the flag, who allows the protester to burn the flag.

AMERICA'S FINEST

As I begin this column I am sitting in Narita Airport in Tokyo waiting for a flight to the good old U.S.A.

We left Seoul, Korea, a few hours ago after completing a tour of military bases. We had a great time entertaining some of the finest armed forces in the world—young men and women who have dedicated the cream of their youthful years to the defense and preservation of our way of life.

We rode in Humvees, airplanes, and Blackhawk helicopters and stood at the 38th Parallel which is the jumping-off place for democracy and where communism and all its attendant miseries and injustices begin. It's just an imaginary line across the ground but it separates millions from freedom.

The North Korean people are living in the evil clutches of the world's most repressive communist regime, a totalitarian government which keeps them isolated from the free world, jamming radio and television signals and denying any semblance of a free press.

It makes you so proud to be an American when you stand there looking over into communist North Korea, where the guards take positions not to keep South Koreans out, but to keep the North Koreans in. In fact, the rank and file North Korean citizen is not allowed anywhere close to the demilitarized zone.

There is no doubt in my mind that the Communists would like nothing better than to sweep down through South Korea confiscating the rich farmland and the ultimate prize of Seoul.

There is only one thing which prevents them from doing it. They know they would face the wrath of the United States of America and the Republic of Korea, and that's an awesome enemy.

I wish every American could stand at the 38th Parallel and feel the hostility and understand that it's one of the most volatile places on earth.

It really makes you realize that it's a shame what Bill Clinton has done to our military. We have been lulled to sleep with the demise of the Soviet Union and diplomatic relations with Red China. We have listened to the placating voices of lily-livered politicians telling us that all is well in our world and we don't need a strong defense.

Well, all is not well in our world. There are numerous flash points which serious trouble could begin at the drop of a hat and as things stand now we do not have the armed forces to guarantee victory.

This is a disgrace for America, and we had better wake up to the fact that the decimation of our armed forces is most ill-advised in the world we live in.

It seems that as long as the economy is good, America is willing to go along with just about anything. Lying, cheating, debauchery, and all the other things this administration has exposed us to. And that's bad enough, but when politicians jeopardize the security of this nation for their own selfish political gain, it's downright treachery.

Our men and women in uniform have always been there when we've needed them. Now they need us; will we be there for them?

AN OPEN LETTER TO PRESIDENT GEORGE W. BUSH

Dear Sir,

The other night when you were speaking at a location I can't recall, members of the audience were able to ask you questions, and a young man in a military uniform prefaced his question by saying that he was proud to call you his commander in chief.

I am not in the military, but I'm proud to call you my commander in chief also. Your unabashed stand as a Christian is really inspiring to the rest of your brothers and sisters in Christ Jesus and I thank God that the leader of the free world seeks the guidance of his Creator in running the affairs of the United States of America.

You speak in the vernacular of the common man and it doesn't take a degree in English to understand what you're talking about. You communicate with the boys down at the farmers' co-op, the steel factory workers and even the highbrow, intellectual, highly educated, self-aggrandizing chowder heads who frequent the cocktail circuits of our big eastern cities.

You've surrounded yourself with people of integrity and wisdom, people who have been there, done that, whose advice is garnered from experience and serve because of their capability, not racial quotas and political correctness. The decisiveness, resolve, and tenacity you have demonstrated in conducting the war against terrorism is truly exemplary. Your courage and your "buck stops here" attitude even further enhance your qualifications as a great leader.

I think that Washington and the mainstream media are a little bewildered by the boldness with which you speak. Everybody with half a brain knows that North Korea, Iran, and Iraq are volatile, dangerous countries, but when you have the guts to say it and issue a "Don't tread on me" warning, they accuse you of everything from being insensitive to warmongering.

Well, sir, it's time somebody stood up and told the American people the bottom line truth. No word-parsing, no back-tracking, no wondering what the meaning of the word "is" is. Just the plain old Gospel truth, whether it be good or bad.

I almost feel as if I know you, sir. I've cleaned up brush, spent a lot of time in the woods hunting, and share your love for wide open spaces and dogs. You came from good stock; I had the privilege of meeting your father on several occasions and I think he was a great president and is a great man.

I applaud you for having the intestinal fortitude to say that a fetus is an unborn child. The "save the whales and kill the babies" crowd are shivering in their boots, afraid that the truth about abortion is going to dawn on the American public, and maybe even some of the adolescent politicians who walk the halls of Congress.

Don't worry too much about how the media treat you. They are an incestuous bunch; they sit in their ivory towers and pontificate instead of reporting, only associate with others of their ilk, and know next to nothing about what's going on in the heartland. They don't understand you and they fear you because the rank-and-file citizenry not only supports you but we trust you and love you.

You are our man, you are one of us, and as they'd say in your home state of Texas, "We're mighty proud of you."

You are in my prayers. May almighty God comfort and guide you as you pursue the awesome task of leading this nation.

REFLECTIONS ON THE FOURTH

As I sit here writing this column it is the Fourth of July and our nation is celebrating her 225th birthday. It's a thought provoking day to say the least.

As I think about that handful of brave men who got together in 1776 and forged a document to King George of England telling him that we would no longer live under English rule, we would no longer pay his taxes, we would no longer be his subjects. These men were not just signing a piece of paper, they were laying everything they had, including their lives, on the line.

For when King George read the Declaration of Independence he declared them all traitors to the crown and decreed that they should all be hanged. I'm sure when the king received this document so eloquently worded by Thomas Jefferson he must have thought, "How dare this upstart colony, this pimple on the face of the new world, invoke the wrath of the mighty British Empire, with its vast armies and monolithic navy! Why, we'll just send a few of our crack troops over there and show them who's boss. This shouldn't take too long."

And by all logic he should have been right. America had no standing army, a few militiamen were pretty much it so far as an organized military was concerned. We had no vast stores of muskets, gunpowder, and cannonballs. So I'm sure King George and his officers thought that whipping America back into line would be little more than spanking an unruly baby.

But there were a few things King George hadn't counted on. One being the American spirit: "Give me liberty or give me death. . . . I regret that I have but one life to lose for my country." The attitude of a people who would live free or die trying.

He didn't count on the tenacity and faith of a George Washington nor the boys from Tennessee and Kentucky who could knock a squirrel's eye out from fifty yards, and would hide behind the trees and pick off his Redcoats.

He didn't know about Francis Marion, the wily Swamp Fox, whose hit and run tactics harassed the British troops at every turn. He just didn't understand that this new nation had a will of its own and would fight to the last man to preserve its precious liberty.

As we all know, we won the Revolutionary War and became the United States of America. We would climb many mountains as a nation. We would go through a Civil War and it would take us almost two centuries to recognize that all men really are created equal. We would lose our sons on the battlefields of Europe, Asia, and Vietnam.

But through it all, by the grace of almighty God, we would somehow preserve our national unity when the chips were down.

When I think of a bloody soldier walking barefoot in the snows of Valley Forge to give us the right to vote, and I think about all the people who are too apathetic or just too lazy to go to the polls, it just plain makes me mad.

When I think about the rope going around Nathan Hale's neck and this brave man dying to give us independence, and I think about politicians who so cavalierly turn our military forces over to the United Nations, it makes me angry.

When I think about the lily-livered, self-serving, power-grabbing, pompous gasbags who walk the halls of our nation's capitol, it just plain makes me want to throw up.

When I think that a handful of pagan lawyers who call themselves the American Civil Liberties Union are trying to strike every vestige of almighty God from every document, every school, every public facet of American life, it makes me all the above.

I urge all you believers to pray for America. Please pray for our leaders and that God will raise up brave, honest people who will help put this nation's feet back on the paths of righteousness.

"As He died to make men holy, let us live to make them free."

SUMMERTIME

Well, it's upon us, summertime. With all its good points like fresh vegetables and outdoor activities, and all its bad points like sweltering temperatures and mosquitoes.

It's time for charcoal, sunscreen, and insect repellent, time for baseball and bass fishing, Vidalias and vacations, sunburn and strawberries.

It's time to break out the swimsuits and the barbecue grill, time to head for the mountains or the seashore or whatever suits your fancy.

Time for the yearly sabbatical of running from pillar to post trying to pack a year's worth of sightseeing into two weeks, determined to have a good time even if it kills you.

I sometimes think that we work harder at our vacations than we do at our jobs.

We get up at ridiculous hours to catch crowded planes to crowded destinations, humping mountains of luggage and paying inflated prices for hotel rooms and snow cones.

We drive down interstates inundated with cars, vans, and sports utility vehicles all feverishly hogging the passing lane so they can get to Florida five minutes earlier to stand in line at Disney World.

We get up early in the morning, pack every possible inch of our cars with baggage and kids, and spend the day listening to the old adage, "When are we going to get there?"

We get back home from our vacations needing a vacation to rest up from our vacations.

We go back to work with suntans and snapshots and bore our fellow workers with sterling accounts of what we did while we were hurrying around the country eating fast food and staying in motel rooms where the air conditioning doesn't work.

But who cares about the sunburn and the depleted bank account? And nobody minds a little sand in the suitcase. After all, it's summertime. Time for fun in the sun.

And what's a picnic without rain? And if we have to sweat through a heat wave, it's no big deal.

And if she wants you to cut the grass on a Saturday afternoon when the Braves are playing a doubleheader on television, so what?

And did you ever notice how summertime limits our inhibitions? What other time of year could you get a fifty-year-old man to walk around shirtless with his belly hanging over the belt line of his Bermuda shorts, or get an otherwise conservative woman to stuff herself into a skimpy bathing suit?

With all its hassle and hustle its a wonderful time and probably the most anticipated season of the year.

Summer means freedom. School's out, the world is in bloom, and as the poet so succinctly put it, a young man's fancy lightly turns to thoughts of love.

And no season passes as quickly as summer. It seems that we've just finished off the Fourth of July watermelon when Labor Day rolls around, and just like a wisp of smoke, summer packs up her bright colors and her good times and leaves us with nothing but memories. Wonderful, pleasant memories.

FAIR

Every year we play quite a few county, regional, and state fairs, and last night in Columbus, Indiana, we started our fair season.

Before the show I took pictures with several fresh-faced young ladies wearing sashes emblazoned with "Miss So-and-So" identifying them as local beauty queens. They were gracious and lovely and seemed to appreciate being chosen for their positions.

There were kids in the audience fresh from the show barns where they had hopefully exhibited their prized heifer or pig.

The fairs are where you see the whole family at the show, all sitting together while everybody helps restrain young Tim or Tina who is more interested in the bright lights than the music and will more than likely fall asleep halfway through "Long Haired Country Boy."

As you stand on the stage you can see the Ferris wheel and the taller rides on the Midway and between songs you can faintly hear the sounds of the hurdy-gurdy carnival music and if the breeze is stirring you can catch the occasional whiff of onions sizzling on a grill.

There's just something very American about fairs. There's something for everybody from the youngest to the oldest.

The ladies bring their finest canned goods and fanciest patchwork quilts all vying for the blue ribbon, while the men display their finest livestock and participate in tractor pulls and the like.

Of course, the main attraction for the kiddies always has been and always will be the Midway. It's the middle American equivalent of the yellow brick road. The spinning wheels and colored lights intermingled with the smell of popcorn is enough to fill any young mind with excitement. The occasional pair of teenagers walk hand in hand with the first blush of young love coloring their smooth cheeks. More concerned with holding hands than with what's going on around with them, they laugh at nothing at all and steal kisses at the top of the ferris wheel.

The old men stand in clumps of three or four and talk about politics or the good old days when it only cost a dime to get into the fair. The adolescent young men walk by and cast wistful glances at the scantily clad ladies on the stages of the girlie shows and wonder what happens when you go inside.

An engaged couple stand at a booth where the young man has spent half of his week's pay trying to win that cute teddy bear for his fiancée . . . just one more try.

For one week a year the fair rolls into town and turns a vacant field into a multicolored, candy coated, loud and rowdy wonderland, spellbinding the young and fascinating the old, and then one morning it's gone leaving behind only windblown trash and the faint scent of cotton candy.

And maybe just maybe a bit of nostalgia for a day gone by when entertainment was a family affair, before television became the centerpiece of our lives and things weren't so dad-blamed complicated.

FARMING

One of the hardest-working and least appreciated segments of our society are our farmers. I speak from experience, limited experience admittedly, as I chose the fiddle instead of the plow, but nevertheless I've had a taste of it.

Farming is the chanciest, most aggravating way to make a living, but still the most rewarding and wonderful way of life.

Farmers are at the mercy of the weather, international markets, and the whims of a body of politicians in Washington who know about as much about farming as a hog knows about an airplane.

I remember getting up at two o'clock in the morning to get the work done on my uncle's tobacco farm in North Carolina. It was just something that had to be done, and if anybody realizes the urgency of getting something done on time it's a farmer.

My grandfather raised nine children on a small farm without electricity or running water.

They raised a lot of their own food, canning vegetables and salting down pork. They had corn ground into meal and a cow supplied milk and butter.

There was a code of responsibility on a farm. Everybody had to pull his own weight and if you messed up, which I did quite often, it was evident to one and all.

Our farmers are stout-hearted individuals. The uncertainty of the profession would completely unnerve lesser men.

There are years of not enough rain, too much rain, drought and cloudburst, and it seems that every bug type critter known to man think that they have a right to part of the crop.

Farming is a sunup-till-sundown proposition, day in, day out, year in, and year out.

Farmers have no paid vacations, no unions, no company retirement plans, and no golden parachutes.

One of the saddest things happening in farming today is the disappearance of the family farm. That's the life I remember and cherish.

I remember a time when we worked hard five-and-a-half days a week, but at twelve o'clock on Saturday we headed for town, along with 90 percent of the other farm families in Bladen County, North Carolina.

Saturday was a day for movies and chocolate sodas, for grocery shopping and socializing. Just about the biggest event in a country boy's life.

The streets of Elizabethtown, North Carolina, would be jammed with cars and pickup trucks and the sidewalks were jammed with people.

The barber shop was always full and you had to wait your turn to get a haircut, which I only did when parentally threatened.

We went to Sunday school on Sunday, and Sunday dinner, which is the midday meal in North Carolina, was fried chicken, the best you ever put in your mouth.

Some of the best meals I ever remember having were at my Aunt Lois's table, good, hearty fare, and plenty of it, with homemade biscuits and fresh country butter.

In those days I never knew anybody who didn't believe in God. Who didn't respect the flag.

The boys and girls raised on those family farms had morals, a sense of responsibility and a dedicated work ethic.

Some went on to college and became doctors, lawyers, and engineers.

Some fought our wars and manned our assembly lines.

But a few went back to the farm, back to a life of hard work and uncertainty. Back to a life of being your own boss, setting your own pace, and seeing more sunrises in a year than most people see in a lifetime.

Back to raising respectful, God-fearing children. Back to the land.

I salute you, all of you who till the land. It is an honorable profession, a truly honorable profession.

THE TIMES THEY ARE A'CHANGIN' AGAIN

As someone who never even watched television until he was fifteen years old, who learned to drive on a stick shift transmission, who used a crosscut saw and a horse-drawn plow, who remembers when a computer took up the biggest part of a couple of good-sized rooms, who has seen the advent of the ballpoint pen, the jet airplane, and hundreds of other mind-blowing things, I must say that it still amazes me when I use a cell phone or watch television rolling down the road via a roving satellite dish.

There's just no keeping up. Technology changes so fast that by the time I get a halfway grasp on something, it is replaced by something newer, faster, and much more complicated—for a mind that has dealt in words and notes for the biggest part of its existence.

I guess what I'm trying to say is that insofar as technology is concerned I feel like a dummy. For instance, I've been wanting an MP3 player and the other day I was in New York City and I figured that would be a dandy place to find one. And I was right. I found plenty of them and bought two.

When I got back home Little Charlie came up to show me how to use them and much to my chagrin said something like, "Dad these are made to be compatible with IBM-type hardware and you've got Apple."

So here I am with several hundred dollars' worth of electronics which I purchased in New York that ain't worth a hill of beans as far as my equipment is concerned. It seems that I'm constantly making those kind of mistakes. I just have a hard time thinking in terms of what software is compatible with what hardware and so forth.

Little Charlie, who is my computer guru, can show me something time after time and it seems that I keep making the same mistakes over and over. I guess it has something to do with old dogs and new tricks.

So much has changed in my lifetime that it's hard to grasp, and for someone who was born in the first half of the twentieth century, it's downright mind boggling.

I remember rotary dial telephones, ice boxes that worked with real ice, and doctors who made house calls. I even remember the days in rural North Carolina when whole segments of the country were without electricity, which meant no washing machines and battery radios.

Don't get me wrong; I have no desire to return to the days of oil lamps and outdoor sanitary facilities. No sir, I'm as attached to indoor plumbing as the next man. And I love having the football games come right into my living room.

It's just that I feel about technology much like I feel about my golf swing. I ain't ever going to be no Tiger Woods, so I'd just best enjoy the game and not get upset when I hit a bad shot, which seems to be about every other one.

In the same way, I'm never going to be a computer whiz, I'll never be able to set the time on my VCR, or program the numbers in my cell phone, and I've just given up on trying to figure out how satellites work.

I'm just going to take my little laptop computer, my remote control, and go on about my life content in the fact that I'm probably not the only dummy in the world.

After all, I may be out of touch with technology but I'm still rockin' and rollin'.

SPORTS

I have had two occasions in as many days to realize how much professional sports has become a significant part of my life. Let me first of all get the sad part out of my way: the tragic and untimely death of Payne Stewart.

I had just walked into the pro shop at the Pumpkin Ridge Golf Course in Portland, Oregon, to play a round and heard the television news was announcing the downing of his plane. It was kind of ironic to learn of his demise at a golf course, and I was a little surprised at the depth of the feelings that I had.

I neither knew, nor had I ever met Payne Stewart, though he had brought me countless moments of enjoyment with his world class golf shots and his wonderful sense of humor.

He was truly one of a kind, one of golfdom's most recognizable personalities, with his knickerbocker trousers and signature cap. You knew who he was from as far away as you could see him.

His perky and articulate way of talking made him a favorite of television announcers and media audiences.

He was a class act and will be missed by the public and by a sport sorely lacking in effervescent personalities.

The second thing that plumbed the depths of my feelings for sports and sports figures happened while I was watching the presentation of the team of the century at the second game of the World Series.

Seeing Hank Aaron, Willie Mays, and Ted Williams on the same stage with Stan the Man and Yogi Berra was touching to say the least, but the highlight of the night for me was to see the crowd in Atlanta give Pete Rose such a rousing round of applause.

I have never felt that it was right to strip Pete Rose of the honors that he earned in baseball.

I don't know the validity or the nonvalidity of the charges against Pete Rose. I do know that he was charged with betting on baseball, although he never bet on or against his own team.

I feel that Pete Rose was a scapegoat, a poorly chosen example who was railroaded out of a game that he dearly loved.

A game which he devoted his life and energy to, a game which he helped to elevate to a higher level.

Yes, Charlie Hustle was quite a ball player and I really hate the raw hand that he was dealt.

My all time favorite baseball player is Hank Aaron. And to see him relive a small measure of the homage he so richly deserves on national television is gratifying to say the least.

All in all it is hard to imagine my life without sports.

How would we spend our Sunday afternoons without our well-paid modern day gladiators going at it? What would October be like without the World Series?

The Masters, the Super Bowl, Wimbledon, and March Madness have all become an integral part of our lives. The Stanley Cup, the Daytona 500 and the National Finals Rodeo all have a place in the heart of the true sports fan.

Speaking for myself and a few million other red-blooded American males, let me just say that the only thing wrong with Monday night football is that it's not a double header.

A GREAT YEAR FOR BASEBALL

What a wonderful year for the nation's pastime. After the strike a few years ago I was so mad at the greed and intractability of the players and owners that I didn't know if I'd ever really get back into baseball ever again.

But time heals even the most stubborn of wounds, and before I knew it, I was right back at the television set rooting for my beloved Atlanta Braves, and cheering Chipper, Javy, Andres, and company on to another winning season.

The caliber of baseball this year has been like nothing I've ever seen. It seems that the players just get faster and stronger and more capable all the time: so many great batting averages, incredible pitching, so many acrobatic defensive plays—and how about them New York Yankees! They've won more games than any other team ever has in a single season. They're awesome.

And the home run production was nothing short of unbelievable, with the old single season home record set by Roger Maris in the sixties being broken by not one, but two men.

And not just ordinary guys either. I feel that Mark McGwire and Sammy Sosa are classy representations of what an athlete should be. Nice guys, who really care about the game, and about the way they comport themselves.

What a great way for it to happen. A black man and a white man, an American and a non-American with respect for each other, respect for the game, and respect for their fans.

And McGwire put to rest that old adage about how many games it took to break the record. He actually did it in fewer games that Babe Ruth or Roger Maris.

It has been a truly wonderful season. We've had the home run record broken, a perfect game pitched, the winningest season ever for a single team, and the Atlanta Braves are back in post-season play, and it just don't get much better than that.

NASCAR RACING

I have received so much e-mail about the tragic death of Dale Earnhardt that I wanted to share my thoughts with those of you who were his fans, and those of you who may not understand what this man meant to the world of racing.

Dale's success as a NASCAR driver is well-documented and there's no need to go into that. Everybody knows that he was a winner and one of the most successful drivers of all time.

I met Dale at the Talladega race last year and he was a true gentleman, courteous and outgoing, with a quick smile and handshake, definitely one of the good old boys.

I know that some people think that we're making a big deal out of this, that people die every day, and after a period of mourning it's time to move on, and you're right.

But, and I say this with the utmost respect, you probably don't understand what NASCAR means to somebody from the southeastern part of the country. The rest of the world has its formula and Indy cars, but the South's got stock car racing and Elvis Presley never had a more rabid fan than some of the gentlemen who risk their lives flying around the track on Sunday afternoons.

This kind of racing began with the moonshine haulers in the mountains of Carolina, on the dirt tracks with old boys who spend the last cent they've got on a new carburetor so they can race Saturday night.

It's not just a sport, it's an obsession, and if you truly want to understand go sit among the shirtless faithful in Charlotte, Atlanta, or Talladega, watch their faces when their favorite driver gets into contention, listen to them roar as the checkered flag is dropped. Sit there with them for one race and you'll learn more about NASCAR and its fans in four hours than you could ever learn reading about it or watching it on TV.

You'll hear about Dale and Darrell and Donnie and King Richard.

Old-timers like Fireball Roberts and Lee Petty and Herb Thomas and his fabulous Hudson Hornet.

These names are heroes to a southern boy and stock car racing is as much a part of our heritage as hominy grits and fried chicken.

So if it seems that some people just can't quite let Dale go, be patient with us, we'll get over it eventually.

But wherever the fast cars roar around the track on a hot Sunday afternoon, when the faithful stand up and cheer their favorites, every time whoever takes the checkered drives down victory lane, Dale Earnhardt will be remembered, cherished, and most of all, missed.

HOW 'BOUT THEM VOLS?

Now don't get the wrong opinion, I'm not bragging—well, maybe I am—well, OK, I'm bragging.

But it ain't everyday that your very favorite football team in the whole world wins a national championship.

It ain't every day that all them East Coast Yankee sports writers have to eat all the disparaging and downright insulting things they've had to say about my beloved Vols all year long.

It ain't every day that the Big Orange team from Tennessee stars on prime time television whipping up on brother Bobby Bowden's Florida State Seminoles, perennially one of the top teams in the nation.

We're number one!!!!! We're number one!!!! Get used to it, Steve Spurrier.

To understand the depth of the feeling for the Tennessee Volunteers football team, you've got to know a little about their fans.

If the Vols were to play on the moon, there would be about 50,000 Tennessee fans there to cheer them on. They're the greatest fans in the world, going wherever their team plays, on planes and cars and caravans of motor homes flying the Big Orange colors.

The Vols have been contending for a national title for the last several years, but this year all the pieces came together.

It's been said that they're a team of destiny, but I don't believe in that stuff. They're just a kick-butt bunch of motivated young athletes with a lot of talent and a ton of heart.

I only got to see one Tennessee game this year. I happened to be off and in town the day they played Vanderbilt in Nashville.

Going to a Tennessee game is a real experience in Knoxville or on the road. As I said, they have the greatest fans in the world, and it's almost like a big happy noisy family.

Tennessee has one of the greatest football traditions in the world. It's the team of Johnny Majors, Reggie White, and Peyton Manning. Of Carl Pickens and Little Man Stewart, just to name a few.

And figure that a little bit of the victory goes to all the people who have been part of the football program at the University of Tennessee.

And if you'd ask them what they thought about it they'd probably say, "How bout them Vols!!!"

SUPER BOWL

I just came back from the Super Bowl in Atlanta where my Tennessee Titans were barely defeated by a great St. Louis Rams team. The game went down to the last few seconds as Super Bowl games should. This was no one-sided match. Both teams were prepared and played their hearts out and the game could have gone either way.

It was just two great football teams slugging it out for sixty minutes, nobody backing up and nobody blinking. Just great football.

In my opinion, there are no losers in the Super Bowl. One team just wins a little more than the other. After all, they are the two teams out of the whole NFL that have won the right to represent their conferences, and every other team in the league would give their eyeteeth to be there.

Tennessee is proud of our Titans. We're proud of the season they've had, we're proud of the individual players and we're proud that they've played in their first Super Bowl. Win, lose, or draw.

There's just something about a football team that pulls a community together. Something everybody can have in common, in spite of whatever other differences they have.

My son, Charlie, has become a Titan fanatic. He knows the players' names, the status of their injuries, and their individual value to the team. He eats, sleeps, and drinks Titan football and hollers so loud at the games, it's a surprise that he can talk afterward.

But he's one among the many people in this community that have embraced this football team and support it at home and on the road.

It kind of reminds me of another football team we have over in the eastern part of the state called the Tennessee Volunteers, whose Big Orange colors are an intricate part of so many Tennesseans lives.

The support for the Vols, as they are affectionately known, is nothing short of spectacular. They draw in excess of 100,000 to every home game, and their fans will travel anywhere to see their team play, including the moon, if they ever get invited to the Lunar Bowl.

Now, it seems that I sense a similar type of devotion developing for the Titans. I am seeing cars now with a Tennessee Titans flag on one side and a Tennessee Volunteers flag on the other.

It's the Vols on Saturday and the Titans on Sunday, and the Volunteers' National Championship last year and the Titans' Super Bowl appearance this year have done nothing but add fuel to the flame.

I don't know if the magnitude of going to the Super Bowl has dawned on Tennessee yet. How rare and wonderful it really is. How hard our players had to work to get there and the honor it has brought to the great state of Tennessee.

My hat is off to my Christian brother, Kurt Warner, and the St. Louis Rams. They played a valiant game and beat a great team.

But I'll tell you what, fellows, don't get that crown too firmly planted on your heads, because next season is not that far away and those high-flying Tennessee Titans and their rabid fans will be coming after you again.

PART 3
FAITH AND FAMILY

Heart of my heart,
rock of my soul,
You changed my life
when You took control.

—"Heart of My Heart,"
from Steel Witness, 1996

AN OPEN LETTER FROM ONE OF THE RIGHT-WING CHRISTIANS

I am truly amazed at the things I'm hearing on television these days. Things like that John McCain's attack on Pat Robertson and Jerry Fallwell may help him win the primaries in California and New York.

Things like people saying that the Christian Right, whatever that is, has no place in politics and that Christian leaders should stay out of the fray.

Have things gone so far that a politician can malign honorable men who stand up for what they believe in and it will actually help him at the polls?

I shouldn't be surprised. Jesus said that the world would hate us. But I thought that John McCain was a decent man. I have altered my opinion of him considerably.

First of all, he claims to be a Republican, which he is not. He is an opportunist who is actually running against his own party and doesn't seem to care if he tears it apart as long as he can keep riding around on that chartered jet.

Well, Mr. McCain, let me explain something to you and your ilk.

People like Pat Robertson and Jerry Fallwell do the things they do and say the things they say because they believe in them, not to win a popularity contest, or to look good on the evening news.

They base their comments on the inerrant word of God and not on the findings of the latest Zogby poll.

What you call intolerance is a commitment to the high calling of Jesus Christ, and they have a right, actually a responsibility to be involved in politics.

Pat Robertson and his organization do more good in this world than you and all the other ninety-nine senators who speak of high ideals and helping the needy but do precious little to attain it. And when you do manage to get something through both houses of Congress it contains enough pork to sink the Queen Mary.

While you're sitting around trying to figure out how to win your next election Pat Robertson is sponsoring a flying hospital that goes around the world and treats people who would otherwise have little hope of receiving quality health care. And guess what, it's all free.

While you're trying to make the other party look bad, Pat Robertson is feeding the hungry and clothing the naked and leading lost souls into the kingdom of God.

What Al Gore and Bill Bradley call choice is murder. You see, the truth is the truth is the truth, and you can't change it with any amount of rhetoric. And if you don't like that you can get mad at God, although I wouldn't advise it, because it's His word—not mine.

It's strange to me that the people who keep this nation afloat with their pleadings and prayers to Almighty God to spare this country would be criticized and ridiculed. You should be thankful for the praying people of this country.

I want to make it perfectly clear right now. I stand with my Christian brothers and sisters. I will pray for America and her citizens, her sick, her poor, and her unsaved. I'll even pray for her politicians.

THE TEN COMMANDMENTS

I have always enjoyed Andy Rooney's hyperbole and witticisms on *60 Minutes*. He has a knack for making us recognize the downright silliness which exists in our society. But this past Sunday I was really disappointed in Mr. Rooney, who chose as his topic for ridicule the Ten Commandments.

He went through and picked out the ones he thought were relevant to today, modified others and dismissed the rest. Why Mr. Rooney, who I think is probably a decent man, would choose to satirize the unchanging word of God is beyond me.

Of course, Mr. Rooney is not alone; I have heard the Ten Commandments joked about and disrespected by far too many people lately.

I don't know how these people bring themselves to belittle the word of God when the Bible contains a strict warning about adding to or taking away from the Holy Scriptures.

It would scare me to death to ridicule the things which are written in the Bible. I could never do it. I don't want to have to face that in the hereafter.

I can't understand why people are so upset about displaying the Ten Commandments in public places.

A lot of the same people who are so radically pro-choice are just as radically opposed to the public display of the Ten Commandments.

If these people really believed in the right to choose, they would realize that a person could choose to walk right by the commandments and never even glance at them. Freedom of choice, to look or not to look.

The ACLU is adamantly opposed to having the Ten Commandments visible in public places and yet would fight tooth and nail for the right of pornographers to display their sleazy wares just about anyplace they want to.

The People for the American Way are opposed to it also. Their American way must be vastly different from the one established by our forefathers, who had great respect for the Ten Commandments.

This nation is on a collision course with anarchy as it is, as politically appointed liberal judges more concerned with coddling criminals than protecting the rights of the victims turn a blind eye to the decay in our streets, and the system which is supposed to protect us is bogged down in plea bargains and revolving door prisons.

Hollywood doesn't have much respect for the Ten Commandments. They have gone from an industry which once made an epic film about the commandments to an industry which seems to strive to make movies that break all ten of them in a two hour span.

And getting right down to it, can someone please tell me what is wrong with everybody being exposed to the commandments? Is there something wrong with people hearing that they are breaking the laws of God by killing, stealing, lying, committing adultery, and so on?

We have turned from a nation with an indomitable pioneer spirit and a deep belief in God to a race of coddled panty-waist whiners who let a handful of atheists, sleazeball lawyers, and gutless politicians steal our very heritage and imperil our national soul.

And I'm sick and tired of it.

CHRISTIAN MUSIC

I just received another e-mail from someone who came to a concert and was disappointed because I didn't play all Christian music. They said that I should give up playing any kind of music except Christian.

When I first started recording Christian music I was asked by the media and others, "How do you think your fans are going to feel about you recording gospel music?"

To which I replied, "I don't believe they'll think much about it at all since I've included gospel music in my show for years. And besides that, regardless of what anybody thinks I'm going to do it anyway. I had waited a long time for an opportunity to do a Christian album and I believed that it was something I should do."

I have done two Christian albums, *The Door* and *Steel Witness,* and have plans for doing another one later on this year.

I have received some of the most heartwarming mail I have ever received concerning these albums, and our fans, who have been with us for many years, have never criticized us for doing them.

The only people who have been critical have been, believe it or not, Christians. Admittedly, not most Christians. They have been very complimentary about the whole thing.

But once in a while I'll hear from somebody who thinks that I should stop playing secular music altogether.

I simply cannot understand this way of thinking. Why should Christians just completely give all the secular music to Satan? He has enough of it now.

I do a family show, a show you can bring anybody in your family to and they will not be embarrassed or offended.

I know that being in the public eye as I am that I leave myself open to criticism. I expect it, but does it have to come from people who are supposed to be my brothers and sisters? Are they saying that because I play music other than Christian music I don't have a right to be a Christian? Are they saying that I can't serve the Lord and be an entertainer?

Whatever happened to love and understanding and not judging others? How can they judge me when all they see is the tip of the iceberg. How can they know the kind of person I am; how can they see what is in my heart?

I wonder how many baby Christians have left the faith because they could not live up to the expectations of some self-righteous Pharisee who criticizes someone for having a glass of wine and then sees someone in need and does nothing about it?

I wonder how many people have made a decision to follow Jesus only to be chastised by some pompous, stiff-necked person so weighted down by the law that the light of Jesus is completely covered up.

Please don't get me wrong; I don't claim to be the most sanctimonious person in the world and I am not holding myself up as a role model for anyone.

I am just a sinner saved by the grace of God and the blood of Jesus. I have done nothing to earn that salvation nor can I ever do anything to repay the gift of the tiniest drop of Jesus' blood.

But until the day that God makes it clear that He doesn't want me doing what I'm doing, I will be out there playing music for the folks, doing my best to bring some decent family entertainment into a world with way too much of the other stuff.

HEROES

This week of October 15, 1999, will be a very special time for me, as I'll have the honor of being in the presence of one of my biggest heroes, the Reverend Billy Graham.

We will be joining Mr. Graham for an evening of his St. Louis crusade. We will be performing three songs, but the best part is we get to stay around and listen to this incredible man preach the Gospel.

This will be our fourth crusade, and each one has been a joy that I can't articulate. I can say, however, that when I'm there I feel as if I'm exactly where I should be, doing exactly what I should be doing at the time I should be doing it, and people, that's a wonderful feeling.

To sit on that stage when Mr. Graham gives the invitation and watch those thousands and thousands of people draining down the sides of those huge stadiums and walking onto the field to give their lives to Jesus Christ is a truly wondrous experience.

Mr. Graham has been preaching God's word for over fifty years now and there is no way to know how many lost souls he has led to the foot of the cross, but it must number in the millions. He has preached all over the world and attracted some of the largest crowds to ever attend an evangelistic service.

Mr. Graham is over eighty years old and at a time when most people would have been retired for many years he's still traveling around doing God's work. He is humble, plainspoken, friendly and warm, devoid of ego and self-importance, and still speaks with the folksy accent of his native North Carolina.

The first Billy Graham crusade we did was in Charlotte, North Carolina, which is considered Mr. Graham's unofficial home town. The governor of North Carolina and the governor of South Carolina were both there with plaques to present and homage to pay to their revered native son.

I think that although appreciative, he was a little embarrassed by it all and was quick to take the focus off Billy Graham and put it back on Jesus Christ and the reason he had come to Charlotte to begin with.

His messages are so simple, so practical, and so easy to understand, delivered in that straightforward, sincere way that seems to come so naturally to Mr. Graham.

In a world that takes great pride in lampooning anybody who is a professed Christian, Billy Graham is the one exception. You don't hear his name carelessly batted around on Jay Leno or David Letterman.

The respect that the public at large has for this man is boundless. And it's respect which has been earned by Mr. Graham's clean living and spotless reputation. I absolutely cherish every minute that I have been able to spend in the presence of this great man of God, and no, he doesn't have a halo or angel's wings and he doesn't claim to be anything more than a sinner saved by the blood of Jesus through the grace of Almighty God, but I've got to tell you, to me there is something very special about Billy Graham. Something very special indeed.

AN OPEN LETTER TO JANE FONDA

Dear Jane,

I must admit that I was completely taken by surprise when I heard that you had been born again. I never expected to see the day when I could call you sister.

After all, I had some serious problems with what you had done in Vietnam and the liberal stands you have taken on issues.

To be honest, I just didn't like you and I'll confess that I have called you some unflattering names through the years.

I ask you to forgive me for holding these things against you. In fact, I thought you would be one of the last people to accept Jesus.

I realize now that we can never know God's plans and I truly rejoice in your conversion.

If I could, I would like to warn you about some things.

First of all, I think that you will find your relations with the media will be vastly different. Instead of being treated fairly and with favor you can expect to be ridiculed and belittled. You see, the press has a great fear of Jesus and a great distrust for those of us who follow him.

Secondly, I would imagine that a lot of your Hollywood friends are going to treat you much differently. After all, in their eyes it's not cool to be a Christian.

And there will be those in the Christian community who will question your commitment.

Yes, Jane, you're probably going to catch it from all sides, even from people who are supposed to be your friends.

And those who a few short years ago were lauding you with honors and Academy Awards may very well turn their backs on you. So be it. That's just the way of the world.

What you have received is the most precious thing in existence.

What does it profit a man if he gains the whole world and loses his own soul?

So hold on, Jane. Through criticism, ridicule, and doubt. You just keep holding on to Jesus because he is the way the truth and the life. I will be praying for you, Jane. Welcome to the family, my sister.

DAY OF RECKONING

This morning as I was praying I was thinking about how God sent his son to this earth to die the most painful, horrible death that anyone has ever suffered, and I know that Jesus suffered much, much more than anyone else ever has, knowing what kind of world he would be dying for.

A world where innocent children are murdered by the millions and people act as if it was nothing more than swatting a fly.

Where depraved men prey on little children and are turned back out into society again and again.

Where the national media are inundated with shows which routinely defile and belittle the name of God and of Jesus Christ.

Where truth and honor are just words and politicians recklessly risk the future of the greatest nation the world has ever known just to have a few more years in power.

Where common sense is replaced by political correctness. What an immoral, depraved, godless people we have become.

When someone is willing to stand up for God they are ridiculed by the world.

Well, I here and now wish to inform the world at large that I will stand up for God and Jesus Christ and you can ridicule, laugh, criticize, demean, and ostracize me and I will still make my stand.

A time is coming when money, power, fame, and material wealth will mean less than nothing. There is only one thing that will outlast the storm to come, and that one thing is faith in God through the sacrifice of his son, Jesus Christ.

And it is not for sale; it is absolutely free.

When I think about the craven abortionist, the child molesters, the panty-waist politicians and those who condone them, my first emotion is anger. Then when I stop and think about it I feel pity.

Can you imagine Patricia Ireland defending a woman's right to choose to God? Can you see Madeline Murray O'Hair explaining to God why there shouldn't be prayer in school? Can you envision some apostate minister explaining why the Bible doesn't really mean what it says?

Can you see the Supreme Court justices explaining the Constitution to almighty God?

Sound far-fetched? Not at all. In fact, it's going to happen one of these days. These people, as we all must, will have to give account for the way we've lived our lives.

We have all sinned and fallen short of God's standards but Jesus shed His blood as a covering for our sins. This covering is absolutely free and available to every human being ever born.

It is accepted by repenting or turning away from our sins, believing in the Deity and sacrifice of Jesus and verbally asking Him into your heart and life.

So instead of anger at the people who mock God and his laws we should be praying that they find Jesus. The alternative is horrible and eternal.

If there's anyone who reads this and doesn't understand the way to salvation through Jesus Christ, get in touch with me by e-mail and I will send you some literature or put you in touch with someone who will gladly explain it to you and lead you to the Lord. Please include an address.

COLUMBINE

An open letter to Mr. and Mrs. Bernall of Littleton, Colorado, whose daughter, Cassie, was senselessly and wantonly murdered in the Columbine High School massacre when she admitted to being a Christian:

First of all, let me say that this letter contains no rhetoric, no self-proclaimed wisdom, no insincere efforts to rationalize the causes of this incredible disaster.

It is simply a humble attempt to express my personal and heartfelt gratitude to a family which has suffered a loss of indescribable proportions. I send my most heartfelt condolences although I know that any attempt at solace would be woefully inadequate and only Almighty God can bind the deep wounds that you have sustained.

I just want to thank you for raising a daughter who was so grounded in her faith that she was willing to pay the ultimate price for her beliefs. A daughter who had the courage to look Satan in the eye and stand her ground for Jesus Christ.

I, as a Christian, have wondered, "If that had been me facing that gun how would I have reacted, would I have stood tall as she did and proclaimed my love for my Savior or would I have remained silent and hoped that the maniacal eye of the killer would pass me by?"

Until the day we get to heaven we'll never know the ramifications of this single act of faith. How many people have been inspired by her bravery? How many Christians have questioned the depths of their commitment and how many non-believers have wondered what it is about Jesus that's worth dying for?

How many politicians and ACLU lawyers have had to secretly second-guess their commitment to keeping prayer and the Ten Commandments out of our schools?

How many parents have hugged their children, thankful to have them home safely and aware of the fact that they are daily in harm's way? How many young people have been affected by her example?

And all of us have had to be reminded how fragile and uncertain life really is, that there is a hereafter where we will spend eternity in abject misery or unspeakable joy. That the only thing that we can truly rely on is God, and that we should never deny Him even when the cost is high.

So, Mr. and Mrs. Bernall, I thank you for the daughter that you raised and for the example that she has set for all of us.

No war hero has ever shown more bravery than this one precious teenage girl. No Medal of Honor winner deserves more homage or to be more fondly remembered.

I know you miss your daughter. I know that the price she paid was high, but, oh, the reward.

I like to think that Jesus was smiling as the holy angels escorted her into His presence. I like to think that He gave her a great big hug and said, "Welcome home, my good and faithful servant, enter into the joy which was prepared for you before the world began," and then I like to think that He introduced her all around, for His word says that if we'll acknowledge Him on earth, He'll acknowledge us in heaven. And if anyone ever acknowledged Him on earth it was your daughter.

God bless your family and God bless America.

THE OTHER COMMANDMENT

Just before Jesus went to the Cross he gave his disciples another commandment, to love one another.

With the exception of the commandment to love God with all our hearts, the others are all wrapped up in the new one that Jesus gave.

If we love one another we will not steal from each other, kill each other, or sleep with our neighbor's wife. We will honor our parents and keep all the other commandments just by simply keeping this one.

It really came home to me that what is lacking in this world is love.

A lot of things which are done under the guise of love and caring are motivated by basic instincts. Social programs which are instituted for political gain have nothing to do with love and actually smack of servitude. So many of what should be our finer endeavors are fueled by profit not love.

Even in the Christian community where love is supposed to abound we have some serious shortcomings. We sometimes become so critical of other people that we tend to forget that the first thing we're supposed to do is love that person, not judge him.

Are you afraid to tell someone you love them? I don't mean your spouse or your kids; I mean a friend or associate. Are you afraid that you'll be looked upon as silly and weak if you speak those three little words?

Are you afraid that the world will view you as foolish? Well, you're right, they probably will, but who cares?

Try it, just think of someone whom you love and just walk right up and say, "John, I don't think that I've ever told you this, but I love you, not in some twisted sexual way, but as a brother loves a brother." It may seem a little strange the first couple of times but it gets easier and easier.

I tell people that I love them all the time, and I do, and if the world wants to make something out of it they can talk to God about it. It's his commandment, not mine. I'm just simply trying to follow it.

Another thing I do is hug people. There is nothing in this world which takes the place of a good hug. Everybody needs one once in a while. There's something healing in hugging.

I've hugged saints and sinners, bikers, bankers, lawyers, liberals, dopers, cowboys, and a young man dying with AIDS. I even hugged a president one time.

You see, I believe that love can be contagious. I believe that if we really and sincerely show love for others that we can start an epidemic, and oh what a wonderful disease it would be.

If you're having trouble understanding what I'm talking about let me give you a good starting place. The next time you look at someone, don't think about how that person's dressed or how they wear their hair or what color they are or what social strata they belong to.

Look at that person as someone who Jesus spent three hours on the cross for, in unimaginable agony that they might have eternal life. Now, if God loved that person that much, who are we to criticize and judge?

Let's try to develop tolerance and patience with each other. You'd be surprised how far a little courtesy can go. Even if someone is being rude to you, as hard as it is, if you'll be polite and courteous to that person you'll feel much better for it.

Can we try something? You and me? Let's go out today with the thought of keeping that all important commandment to love one another. Let's take that attitude on every drive, into every business meeting, in everything we do and every relationship we have.

Try it for a month sincerely and regularly and see what happens. I think you'll be surprised.

Let me hear from you on this after the month is over.

KINDNESS

It seems as time goes by, we get a little more impatient, a little quicker to anger, and a little less kind to each other. You see it every day from the guy who cuts you off in the passing lane to the teenager who works at the hamburger place who shoves your change at you without so much as a thank-you.

Being polite is so much easier than being abusive and abrasive. It not only makes people like to be around you, it's just better on your blood pressure.

Sometimes a kind word can mean more than we'll ever know to someone who is having a bad day. Even a simple smile can be uplifting to someone who hasn't seen one in a while.

I remember a more genteel time when manners and courtesy were the order of the day, when children showed respect for their elders, a day when corporal discipline was universal in the raising of a child, and no one dared to talk back to a schoolteacher, and a man wouldn't even think of using an off-color word in the presence of a lady.

What happened? Well, in my opinion, manners and courtesy are just two more victims of an overly permissive society.

Good people stood by and let one pitiful atheist have prayer removed from our public school system, and you can say what you want to about that, but we didn't have murders in our schools back in those days. Coincidence? I think not.

We didn't take it seriously when they banished the nativity scenes and Ten Commandments from public places.

Belligerence, arrogance, and downright filth spew forth from our television sets—the bottom line being the criterion, thus justifying Beavis and Butthead and their ilk.

My e-mail screen is inundated with unsolicited offers of hard core pornography and just the language they use to tout this garbage is enough to make an old salt blush.

We have become a vulgar, undisciplined society standing docilely by while little by little any semblance of decency disappears from the American scene.

However, we can't be responsible for the whole world, but we can be responsible for the little bit of space we occupy and we can make our space a better place. We can filter what comes into our space and edit what goes out of it.

I believe that kindness is contagious and smiles are catching.

Were you ever around an individual who was so up and so positive that it just made you feel good to be in his presence?

Did you ever know someone who just radiated good feelings and the first thing you know you're smiling and laughing and having a fine old time?

It all goes back to the golden rule of treating other people the way we want to be treated.

It's so easy, try it. When you go to work today, speak to that person who never speaks to you. Just a simple "good morning" will do. Smile at the old neighborhood grouch accompanied by something like, "How are you today?" Let someone in line in front of you or give some homeless person a couple of dollars.

Smile at the first ten people you come in contact with and speak courteously to everyone you see. Do it for a few days and you might be surprised at the results.

MY HEALTH

I suppose that a lot of you folks have heard about my recent operation for prostate cancer. I went into Vanderbilt Hospital on November 20 and Dr. Joseph Smith performed the operation. After a two-day stay I went back home, where I am now recuperating.

Although there are still some lab reports which can take up to a couple of months to get back, the preliminary pathology is excellent and Dr. Smith feels that the cancer was contained totally in the prostate and is 100 percent cured.

Although I can't say that it was a pleasant experience, I have to say that it has not been nearly as bad as I had it pictured.

I had known about the surgery for several months, in fact, I had the date scheduled. As the time drew near I grew apprehensive to say the least.

There's just something about getting up before daylight and going into a hospital, putting on a gown, being fitted with an IV and talking to nurses and doctors, knowing that soon you're going to be put to sleep, that is a bit unnerving.

The word cancer is one of the most feared in the English language and knowing that you've got one inside you can be a real source of worry and anxiety.

I knew I couldn't handle it so I turned it over to God. I had heard about peace which passeth all understanding, and I am thankful to say that I experienced it. God went right into the operating room with me. Hazel stayed with me as long as she could and when she finally had to leave and they wheeled me into the operating room, I was calm and in a good mood.

Dr. Smith said, "Are you ready to get this done?" to which I replied, "Let's get it over with," and the next thing I remember they were wheeling me to my room and in my semi-awake state I realized that it was all over.

I was so glad to get back to my darling Hazel; I'm just not much good without her and seeing her face was a wonderful experience.

My son, Charlie, was a welcome sight as were several of my extended family of people who work with me.

I was surrounded by love and friendship.

I've had very little pain and got off the pain medication after a couple of days. Dr. Smith says that I'm not to pick up anything that weighs over ten pounds for six weeks and since some of my guitars weigh more than that I have to be kind of careful. And I'm not supposed to drive for a few weeks but I can live with that.

I have said it before and I'll say it again. As tough as life gets sometimes for the people who are Christians, I can't imagine going through life without God and Jesus Christ. There is no other source of comfort in times of trouble, and I praise God for giving me peace and healing me, for giving me a wonderful wife and son and friends who truly care about me. He is so good.

I would like to say a word to you men, especially those of you who are over fifty. Be sure and have a complete physical once a year and be sure to have your PSA levels checked; it can be done in a blood test and is a barometer for prostate cancer. Early detection and treatment can mean the difference between the cancer spreading to other parts of the body—even life and death.

A trip to the doctor once a year can literally save your life.

I want to thank you folks for all the prayers and get-well cards and wishes. I love you all and, God willing, look forward to many more years of playing my music for you.

SIMPLE THINGS

I sometimes reflect on the fact that with all the hustle and bustle, job pressure, peer pressure and blood pressure, the traffic, the crime rate, and all the bad news we see on television, that we just get caught up in the daily grind and simply forget to look around and enjoy the simple things.

For instance, I was driving by Roger and Terry's place today and Terry was out in the yard grooming one of the most beautiful sorrel fillies I've ever laid my eyes on.

Ordinarily I may have just driven on by and never stopped to admire this lovely and gentle creature, but I stopped and petted and admired her.

Hazel is always wanting me to walk around the yard with her to look at her flowers. It's easy to say, "I just ain't got time," but I do it, and a pleasant stroll it is among the roses and all the other flowers I can never remember the names of.

How long has it been since you've been fishing or stopped to watch the sun dip below the horizon? How long since you've held a baby or walked in the rain or played with a puppy? When's the last time you did something silly or sat down to have a serious conversation with a senior citizen? When did you last admire the stars or sleep outside or go to a high school basketball game?

Did you ever walk across the grass early in the morning when the dew was heavy and feel its natural coolness under your feet?

Did you ever go down to a creek and just sit there and watch the water run?

Have you ever seen a newborn colt get on its feet for the first time, still damp from birth and all gangly and awkward? Have you ever seen a red-tailed hawk wheeling lazy circles in a clear afternoon sky?

Did you ever see a herd of white-tailed deer jump a fence or a wild turkey trot down a wooded path? Did you ever hear a lovesick whippoorwill pouring his heart out on a night when the moon is full and the breeze smells like honeysuckle? Did you ever feel a large mouth bass on the end of your line and watch him break the surface and make the water roll, or did you ever hear a bunch of bullfrogs trying to outdo each other around a placid moonlit pond?

How long has it been since you've pulled out your favorite old records and just sat there enjoying them? When's the last time you had a fried apple pie or made homemade ice cream or been in a snowball fight or hugged a good friend and told them just how much they mean to you?

Do you ever roast a hot dog over an open fire or play softball with a bunch of kids or spend your vacation at home?

Life is so beautiful; it can't be relived or rewound. One of these days when you spend more time in a rocking chair than you do behind a steering wheel and you start pulling out those old memories, I'll just bet you a dollar to a doughnut that your favorite ones won't be about the most money you ever made or the social status you achieved or the accolades which have come your way. I'll bet it will be the memory of simple things which will warm your heart through the golden years.

We all tend to get too busy, too stressed out, too focused to stop and smell the roses.

What we need to do is slow life down, try to enjoy every minute of it no matter what we're doing, and get rid of the things in our lives that cause us worry and anguish.

Look around you at this beautiful world.

"Be still and know that I am God."

SHOPPING

When I go shopping I walk into a store and say something like, "Have you got this in my size?" If the answer is yes I'll say something like, "OK, I'll take the red one," pull out my wallet, pay the bill, and walk out of the store with my purchase.

Even to do this is just short of drudgery for me. In other words, except for a very few exceptions, I hate shopping. That's right; that's what I said. I hate shopping.

Traipsing up and down the corridors of some shopping center or looking for a parking place downtown is just not my favorite way of spending time and is just a few cuts below the root canal category in my druthers list.

I also hate buying new cars, trying on clothes, picking out furniture, and everything associated with it. The very thought of Christmas shopping can throw me into a virtual tailspin.

Now Hazel is the direct opposite of me. She loves shopping.

They seldom have a place to sit down in the places Hazel so loves to frequent, and after standing there for what seems like hours she finally finds something she likes, and just as I'm reaching for my wallet she says something like, "No, I really don't care for the bow on the back. Do you have it without the bow?"

Of course they don't have it without the bow, which instigates a whole new search for the perfect elusive outfit which doesn't have that confounded bow. Heck, I could have taken my pocket-knife and cut the bow off the dad-blamed thing.

But no, it's time to go through more racks and racks of garments, and likely not finding anything among the thousands available which suit her, she says the dreaded anticipated words, "Let's go to Green Hills Mall," and we're off to the other side of town where hopefully they have something that suits her fancy.

Shopping is a female sport, from my point of view. It's just something in the feminine genes that drives them on from shopping center to shopping center, taking great delight in dragging their disgruntled spouses along.

They thrive on cross-town traffic and clogged parking lots.

The sight of a sale sign throws them into a frenzy of shopping mania. Armed with their plastic money they descend on the department stores like a swarm of locusts, fingering fabric, trying on blouses and trying to fit an eight-sized foot into a seven-and-a-half-sized shoe. They browse acres of storefronts with the astute eye of an eagle always on the lookout for the reduced price or the buy-one-get-one-free notices.

And you know what the funny thing is? I actually think that the buying is secondary to the shopping. If women could just pick up the phone and have the perfect product delivered, the perfect fit, the perfect color, at the absolutely best price ever made available on Planet Earth, do you really think that they would do that?

I don't; I think they would still drive twenty-five miles through rush hour traffic and go across town to some store with an ad in the Sunday paper advertising some kind of sale.

I think they would still try on dozens of garments and very possibly not buy any of them.

A word of advice to you husbands. When your wife wants you to go shopping with her, grab a good book, find yourself a comfortable sitting down place and say, "Just take your time, dear; I'll be right here when you finish shopping." Grab a cup of Starbucks and relax.

IS IT GOOD FOR THE CHILDREN?

Some time back I was visiting an acquaintance and we started talking about children. He said something that really got me to thinking. He said that everything that is done in this country should take into consideration how it would affect the children, or as he put it, "Is it good for the children?"

When you think about things in that light they take on a whole new meaning. For instance, when legislation is passed we should be concerned about how it will affect the little ones. When a criminal is sentenced or a medicine is approved we should take into account how it's going to affect the children.

When we do environmental impact studies we should do studies to determine the impact on our children. We have been fairly vigilant in civil rights and protecting minorities while for far too long the most helpless segment of our society goes without notice.

They are abused and neglected and brought into the world by people who have no intention of caring for them. Too often when a child abuser is brought to justice the court is more concerned with the rights of the criminal than with the rights of the child, never really considering the horrible fact that a helpless human being has been scarred for the rest of his or her life.

Politicians make education a political football, a way of garnering votes, catering to the teachers' unions and the powers that be rather than taking into consideration how well-educated our future generations will be.

The television networks and Hollywood filmmakers fill our theaters and airwaves with filth, trash and mindless drivel, not even caring what it does to impressionable young minds. It's the bottom line which motivates these people with precious little attention to scruples and morals.

Food manufacturers make and advertise products which they know full well are not healthy for growing children.... Cereals and fast foods with advertising campaigns designed to catch the eye of little people who know nothing at all about nutrition.

The worst kind of neglect is that practiced by parents, and I'm not talking about the scumbags who abuse and refuse to support their offspring. We all know about them; we read about them in the newspapers all the time.

The parents I'm referring to are good people, who work hard to support their families but get their priorities out of whack.

And before some of you start firing off irate e-mails, let me explain myself. I am the first one to realize that there are a lot of situations in this country which absolutely require both parents to have a job.

But there are many cases where both parents work to provide luxuries and perks, and I don't blame anybody for wanting the finer things in life. But is the second car and the overseas vacation really worth raising a latchkey child who has to fend for themselves for several hours a day?

Never in the history of this planet has there been as much harmful mischief for a child to get into, and as many predators roaming the streets stalking innocents. Maybe when we consider a move to another town, a job change, or anything else important in our lives, we should ask ourselves this question: Is it good for the children?

HOPE FOR OUR CHILDREN

I recently attended a meeting of the Professional Advisory Board of St. Jude Children's Research Hospital, of which I am a member.

I don't know how much you all know about St. Jude, but it is located in Memphis, Tennessee, and was started by Danny Thomas in the sixties. They treat children with catastrophic diseases of all kinds, children from all over the world.

They are, as the name implies, a research hospital which maintains state-of-the-art facilities and top research scientists in the field of cancer, AIDS, infectious diseases, and any number of illnesses which attack children.

During the meeting we were joined by some of the research staff and brought up to date on some of the things they are working on, which include, among other things, an AIDS vaccine. Incredible strides in pediatric medicine have been made in recent years by these outstanding people. They are brilliant and devoted and the things they have on the drawing board are absolutely astounding. There is no way that I can convey all the wonderful things which were revealed to the board but I can tell you that it is mind-boggling.

For one thing, they have set up a telemedicine capability by which they will be able by means of two-way television to consult with doctors all over the world, virtually go right into the wards and operating rooms, to make recommendations on procedures, medication, and continuing treatment.

Even in its early stages it is already saving lives. They are also setting up a medical library with up-to-date information and the latest techniques which will be accessible by computer for any doctor who needs the information.

Danny Thomas believed that no child should have to die because he could not afford the treatment he needed and that has become a policy at St. Jude. No one is turned away because of lack of funds, and some of these children spend literally years at the hospital. Of course, those who can afford to pay or are covered by insurance are expected to pay, but if the insurance runs out the treatment doesn't.

When a child has an extended stay at St. Jude one family member is furnished with a place to stay, usually with the child. A lot of the treatment is done on an outpatient variety.

I feel so inadequate trying to describe the wonderful things I experienced at St. Jude Children's Hospital. I could tell you that the cure rate is between 70 and 80 percent and growing.

I could tell you that some of the most brilliant and dedicated people in the world are burning the midnight oil in search of the answers to some of the most heartbreaking childhood diseases known to man.

I could tell you about Jessica Turri, the little girl I met who, after three years of chemotherapy, is cured and smiling and living a normal life.

I could tell you many things but I would still not scratch the surface of the incredible work going on at St. Jude Children's Research Hospital.

What I can tell you is that they are expanding the facilities so they can accommodate more people and further their research.

And I can tell you that the yearly budget will soon increase to a half-billion dollars a year on its way to a billion.

And I could tell you that the bulk of that budget comes from small donors. Oh, sure, there are some heavy hitters who contribute millions to the cause, but the major portion comes from working folks who give what they can afford to, whose twenty or fifty-dollar donation combined with the donations of other caring people go to put smiles on the faces and hope in the hearts of children all over the world.

What I'm trying to say is, I don't use this column ordinarily to try to raise money for any cause, but in the case of St. Jude I urge you all to participate in the wonderful thing that's going on in Memphis, Tennessee.

God bless the children.

SALT OF THE EARTH

Recently I went to Florida to do a charity golf tournament and concert for a wonderful place called the Angelus. The Angelus people take care of themselves. It is operated by Dave and Pauline Shaver who have devoted their lives to taking loving care of people who society has all but forgotten.

None of their charges can walk and spend their lives between a wheel chair and bed, totally dependent on others to be fed, dressed, and for even such mundane things as going to the bathroom.

Teenagers, adolescents, older people, they're all represented at the Angelus and they're all welcome. Some of them have been there for years—they have no other place to go except some cold, sterile, state facility where they're little more than a number.

At the Angelus they're individuals, with specific needs. Love abounds on the grounds of the Angelus; so much hugging and gentle talk, it makes you feel good just to go there.

Every year Dave and Pauline and the staff load up all the Angelus gang and head for the Sunday afternoon concert which is part of the event. Nobody has a bigger time than these precious ones. They're always right down front, a constant reminder of what this is all about.

We have been doing the tournament for nine years now and it is truly gratifying to see what has been accomplished with the money we've raised through the years. A list of artists who have come and given their time and talents to make this event successful is impressive and I am thankful to each and every one of them.

Even more impressive is the list of volunteers who devote several days of their lives to the event every year, and the faithful sponsors who year after year contribute thousands of dollars to the cause.

But the real and mostly unsung heroes here are Dave and Pauline and their loyal crew of caretakers who have devoted their lives to the twenty-four-hour-a-day care of the deformed, the indigent, the helpless.

Such love and devotion is rare and precious and so many of the ones they devote their lives to are not even able to say thank you. The hours are long, the pay is short, and their only reward they have is knowing that what they're doing is right and essential and good.

In retrospect, I'll have to say that the yearly Angelus event is America at its best. People working together to help make someone's life better.

There was a recent poll about the most admired people in America. Bill Clinton came out as the most admired man and Hillary Clinton came out as the most admired woman.

If that is an accurate poll, this country is in sad shape, especially when there are people like Dave and Pauline Shaver around.

TRUE SAINTS

We have affiliated our Volunteer Jam tour this year with an outfit known as Habitat for Humanity. I'm sure you've heard of them; they are the people who make it possible for low income families to move into a brand new home.

I have been privileged to go to three of these presentation ceremonies and seen the faces of the people who were receiving these houses, and I'll tell you, friends, it's nothing short of wonderful, seeing these precious people who had no hope of having their own home receive the keys to a brand new house.

As one recipient so succinctly put it, "I've had to move six times since last May and I ain't going to move no more." It's truly a blessing to see this kind of thing happen and I am very impressed with the work that Habitat is doing.

I am even more impressed with the caliber of people involved in the organization. There is a young man by the name of Shane Clark who acts as liaison between us and Habitat. He travels with us, and I've had the chance to spend some time with him. I am completely amazed by this young man. He has given up his whole life to be in service to the poor of this world.

He spent years in India with Mother Teresa caring for the hungry and the dying, serving mankind at a level which few humans ever understand, much less aspire to. The stories he tells are heartbreaking. The number of destitute souls on this planet is absolutely mind-boggling. The need is so great and the resources and workers so woefully inadequate.

It would seem to be a losing battle, an insurmountable task but to people like Shane it's just another mountain to climb and they sacrifice any semblance of private pleasure or personal comfort to take just one painstaking step at a time.

Jesus said that what we did to the least of these, his brothers, we were doing unto Him. He even mentions giving a cup of water to a child.

Shane has told me stories about Mother Teresa, about how she rose at four o'clock every morning, about a place of prayer where a crucifix hung with the words "I thirst" close by. About Mother Teresa's motto, "I live to quench His thirst." I guess she felt that as long as one person was thirsty Jesus was thirsty, that if one person was hungry Jesus was hungry. She saw others' needs as Jesus' needs, others' pain as our Savior's pain.

Talking to this special young man has given me a whole new view of Christianity. I feel so inadequate, so impotent, so un-Christlike.

I feel that all I've ever done pertaining to the Kingdom of God does not boil down to the worth of one day of Shane Clark's service on the mean streets of Calcutta.

And the amazing thing about this unusual young man is the absolute fact that he does not view his service as drudgery, or even sacrifice, for that matter. He takes great joy in doing the dirty and often thankless tasks that most of us would shrink violently away from.

He has held the dying, he has comforted the helpless, and with his own hands fed the teeming masses of hungry children who are more or less invisible to our affluent society.

I love you, Shane Clark. I love you for what you've done, for what you've been, and for what you are. I love you for the humbling realization that insofar as service to Jesus Christ is concerned, I don't even show up as a blip on the radar screen. I love you for making me desire to be a better Christian.

I admire you, young man, above the powerful politicians, above the rich and famous, above the entertainment icons and the haughty doyennes who make the headlines in the society pages for holding this or that charity ball once a year. Because you, Shane Clark, you've made a difference.

THE LAST THANKSGIVING OF THE MILLENNIUM

As we approach Thanksgiving this year I am reminded of so many things that I should be thankful for. Of course, my greatest gratitude goes to God for his gift of Jesus and the salvation of my eternal soul.

And of course, I'm so thankful for my family and the many happy years that Hazel and I have had together, for my son, Charlie, and for the faithful employees who have been with me through good and bad times, and who take such wonderful care of me, and for the members of my band who make my musical life such a pleasure.

To the road crew who are always there rain or shine humping tons of equipment around the country, the drivers who keep the vigil throughout the 100,000 miles we travel every year, my manager, and our office staff who fiercely promote and preserve my career with such efficiency.

I am thankful for the gift of music and my ongoing love affair with entertaining people. And I'm ever so thankful for those people who allow me to entertain them. Of course I'm thankful for all the material things which God has blessed me with, and I'm also thankful for the intangible and simple things which make up a part of the patchwork quilt which is the life of Charlie Daniels.

For the red tailed hawk I saw circling over the back pasture the other day when Thurman and I were riding our horses, for the softness of a baby's cheek, for the view from our front porch, for the turning of the leaves, for the friskiness of a yearling colt on a cold morning, for the frost diamonds sparkling in an early morning Tennessee sun, and for the sunset that I saw the other day in South Dakota.

I am thankful that I live in the greatest country that the world has ever known and the opportunity to try and make it better. I'm thankful for the truths that I have learned, the prejudices which I have overcome and the friends I have made.

I'm thankful for the lovesick whippoorwill who serenades us on the rare summer evenings when we are home. I'm thankful for the way the full moon comes up and shines down across our valley.

I'm thankful for playful puppies, gentle horses, well-mannered teenagers, and the sound of rain on our tin roof.

For the serenity of life in the country and the mayhem of life on the road.

I'm thankful for Hazel's roses, the beautiful willow tree she planted a few years ago, and the flowers she fusses over each spring.

For cornbread and football, four-wheel drives, and catch ropes and horned cows, for the Gary Morton paintings we're blessed enough to own and the wild turkeys who roam our place in such abundance.

I'm thankful for kind words, for a clean joke and a good hug.

For the hummingbirds, the fox squirrels, and the big catfish that I almost landed.

For the two pine trees on Sugar Hill, for spring water, for the wonderful church we go to and the music that Stevie Ray left us.

I'm thankful for the God-given ability to give love and such wonderful people to give it to.

I'm thankful for every breath I breathe, every step I take, every note I play, every time I kiss my wife, every mile I travel in safety.

Yes, I've got a lot to be thankful for. How about you?

THANKSGIVING 2002

As 2002 draws to a close and we approach Thanksgiving Day, the world is in turmoil, but the U.S.A. has not suffered another 9-11 style attack and for that we should be thankful.

The Beltway snipers have ended the lives of many innocent people, but the police have them in custody and we should be thankful for that.

It looks as if we're going to war with a despot who would like nothing better than to destroy us, but we have the military might to win, and for that we should be thankful.

The airwaves are clogged with nay-sayers who take great joy in telling us that our economy is headed south, but the truth is that we'll persevere just like we always have and we should be thankful for that.

We still have free elections in this country and for that we should be thankful.

The danger to America from maniacal suicide bombers and hostile governments is very real, but we still have young men and women who give up part of their lives to protect us from them and we should be thankful for that.

Some of our European allies are turning their backs on us forgetting that if not for the U.S.A. the map of Europe would all be one color, but with the help of the ones who are still loyal, we can still carry on to whatever victories need to be won, and for that we should be thankful.

The events of 9-11-01 have changed the lives of everyone in America forever, but the subways still run, the planes still fly and the football games are still being played and we should be thankful.

While some of the world can't feed itself, the most productive farmers on earth till the most fertile soil on earth and feed and clothe this nation abundantly, and for that we should be thankful.

If we listen to the major media in this country they would have us believe that all the news is bad, but stop and think about this.

Babies are still being born, cancer is being cured, the sun still rises, and a full moon is just as beautiful as ever. The rain still falls, the wind still blows, the bees still make honey, and there's nothing quite like the sight of quietly falling snow.

Music is still being played, books are still being written, and Hollywood even manages to make a great movie once in a while.

Children still play, young boys still flirt with young girls, and old men continue to impart their hard-earned wisdom.

The heart of this nation is still charitable, still caring, still compassionate. A hug is still comforting, a good laugh is still healing, and love still rules supreme.

Eagles still soar, longleaf pine trees still whisper in the breeze, and well water still tastes good, and there's nothing like watching a cork bob in your favorite fishing hole, and for all that I am truly thankful.

The freely given salvation of Jesus Christ is still available to those who sincerely seek it, and for that we should be most thankful.

Thank you, Lord, for the U.S.A., for freedom, for opportunities to live our dreams. For the Rockies and the Smokies, the Atlantic and Pacific, for jostling interstates and quiet country lanes.

Thank you for the mighty cathedrals and the little white chapels. For solace and sustenance, security and salvation.

If God be for us who can be against us?

A CAROLINA CHRISTMAS CAROL

I might as well go ahead and tell you right up front: I believe in Santa Claus. Now, you can believe or not believe, but I'm here to tell you for a fact that there is a Santa Claus, and he does bring toys and stuff like that on Christmas Eve night.

I know, I know. It sounds like I've had too much eggnog, don't it? All I ask is that you wait till I get through telling my story before you make up your mind.

When I was a kid, Christmastime had a magic to it that no other season of the year had. There was just something in the air, something that you couldn't put your finger on, but it was there, and it affected everybody.

It seemed like everybody smiled and laughed more at that time of year, even the people who didn't hardly smile and laugh the rest of the year.

"You reckon it's gonna snow? I sure do wish it'd snow this year. Do you reckon it's gonna?"

Heck no, it won't gonna snow. As far as I know, it ain't never snowed in Wilmington, North Carolina, at Christmastime in the whole history of man. It seemed like everybody in the world had snow at Christmas except us.

In the funny papers, Nancy and Sluggo and Little Orphan Annie had snow to frolic around in at Christmastime. The Christmas cards had snow. Bing Crosby even had snow to sing about. But not one flake fell on Wilmington, North Carolina.

But that didn't dampen our spirits one little bit. Our family celebrated Christmas to the hilt. We were a big, close-knit family, and we'd gather up at Grandma's house every year. My grandparents lived on a farm in Bladen County, about fifty miles from Wilmington, and I just couldn't wait to get up there.

They lived in a great big old farmhouse, and every Christmas they'd fill it up with their children and grandchildren. We'd always stay from the night of the twenty-third through the morning of the twenty-sixth.

There'd be Uncle Clyde and Aunt Martha, Uncle Lacy and Aunt Selma, Uncle Leroy and Aunt Mollie, Uncle Stewart and Aunt Opal, and my daddy and mama, Ernest and Nadine. I won't even go into how many children were there, but take my word for it, there were a bunch.

There'd be people sleeping all over that big old house. We kids would sleep on pallets on the floor, and we'd giggle and play till some of the grown-ups would come and make us be quiet.

All the usual ground rules about eating were off for those days at Grandma's house. You could eat as much pie and cake and candy as you could hold, and your mama wouldn't say a word to you.

My grandma would cook from sunup to sundown and love every minute of it. She'd have cakes, pies, candy, fruit, and nuts setting out all the time, and on top of that, she'd cook three big meals a day. I mean, we ate like pigs.

Christmas was also the only time that my granddaddy would take a drink. It was a Southern custom of the time not to drink in front of small children, so Granddaddy kept his drinking whiskey hid in the barn. When he'd want to go out there and get him a snort, he'd say that he had to go see if the mare had had her foal yet.

It was a good, good time. A little old-fashioned by some people's standards, but it suited us just fine.

If I'm not mistaken, it was the year I was five years old that my cousin Buford told me that there wasn't any Santa Claus. Buford was about nine at the time. He always was a mean-natured cuss. Still is.

Well, I just refused to believe him. I said, "You're telling a great big fib, Buford Ray, 'cause Santa Claus comes to see me every Christmas, right here at Grandma and Granddaddy's house."

"That ain't Santa Claus. That's your mama and daddy."

One thing led to another and I got so upset about the prospect of no Santa Claus that I went running into the house crying.

"Grandma, Grandma! Buford says there ain't no Santa Claus! There is a Santa Claus, ain't they, Grandma?"

"Of course there is, Curtis. Buford was just joking with you."

Aunt Selma heard me talking to Grandma and walked to the door. "Buford Ray, get yourself in this house right this minute!"

When he came in, Aunt Selma grabbed him by the ear, led him into the front room, and swatted him.

Granddaddy was also a big defender of Santa Claus. He would talk about Santa Claus like he was a personal friend of his. And the more he went to check on the mare, the more he talked about Santa Claus, or "Sandy Claws," as he called him.

"Yes, children, old Sandy Claws will be hitching up them reindeers and heading on down this a-way before long. Wonder what he's gonna bring this year?"

He'd have us so excited by the time we went to bed that I reckon if visions of sugarplums ever danced in anybody's heads, it was ours.

Christmas Eve night, after we had eaten about as much supper as we could hold, we'd go in the front room. There'd always be a big log fire crackling in the fireplace, and Granddaddy would always say the same thing.

"Children, do y'all know why we have Christmas every year?"

"Cause that's when the Baby Jesus was born."

"That's right. We're celebrating the Lord's birthday. Do y'all know where He was born at?"

"In Bethlehem," we would all chime in.

"That's right, He was born in a stable in Bethlehem almost two thousand years ago."

Then Granddaddy would put on his spectacles and read Saint Luke's version of the Christmas story. Then, after we'd had family prayer, Granddaddy would always get a twinkle in his eye. "I reckon I'd better step out to the barn and see if that old mare has had her baby yet."

There was always a chorus of, "Can I go with you, Granddaddy?"

"Y'all had better stay in here by the fire. It's mighty cold outside. I'll be right back."

When Granddaddy came back in the house, he'd always say, "I was on my way back from the barn a while ago, and I heard something that sounded like bells a-tinkling, way back off yonder in the woods. I just can't figure why bells would be ringing back in the woods this time of night."

"It's Santa Claus! It's Santa Claus!"

"Well, now, I never thought of that. I wonder if it was old Sandy Claws. You children better get to bed. You know he won't come to see you as long as you're awake."

Then it was time to say good night. All the grandchildren would go around hugging all the grown-ups. "Good night, Grandma, good night, Granddaddy, good night, Uncle Clyde, good night, Aunt Mollie," and so forth.

We would always try to stay awake, lying on our pallets until Santa Claus got there, but we always lost the battle.

It sounded like the Third World War at Grandma's house on Christmas morning. There was cap pistols going off and baby dolls crying, and all the children hollering at the top of their lungs.

By the time the next school year started, I was six years old and in the first grade. I kept thinking about what Buford had said. I didn't want to believe it, but it kept slipping into the back door of my mind.

At school, Buford was three grades ahead of me, but I'd still see him sometimes. Every time he'd see me that whole year, he'd make it a point to rub it in about Santa Claus.

He'd do something like get me around a bunch of his older buddies and say, "Hey, you fellers, Curtis still believes in Santa Claus." And they'd all laugh and point.

Away from any adult persuasion, I guess Buford finally wore me out. I returned to Grandma's house the next year not believing that there was a Santa Claus. Christmas lost a little of its mystique. Oh, I still enjoyed it. I even pretended that I believed in "Sandy Claws" for Granddaddy's benefit, but it wasn't the same.

Well, as you know, time marches on, children grow up and leave home, including me.

I was living in Denver, Colorado, married, with a child, and I hadn't been home for Christmas since our little daughter had been born. Dawn was three that year, and this would be the first time that she really knew about Santa Claus, and she was some kind of excited.

We had the best time shopping for her, buying all the little toys that she wanted.

Daddy called me about three weeks before Christmas and said, "Son, you know that your grandparents are getting old. They've requested that all the children, grandchildren, and great-grandchildren come home the way we used to. Can you make it, son?"

"We'll be there, Daddy."

I couldn't think of a better place in the whole world for little Dawn to spend her first real Christmas, so we packed up and headed for North Carolina.

Grandma was eighty-two years old, but she still cooked all day long, and she still enjoyed every minute of it. Granddaddy was eighty-four, but he still had a twinkle in his eye and a mare in the barn.

The old house was fuller than ever, with a whole new generation of children in it. Even Buford. He had married, but he didn't have any children. He didn't want any. One of my cousins said he figured Buford was too stingy to have children.

Buford was still the same, except that he had changed from a boy with a mean nature to a full-grown man with a cynical nature and a know-it-all attitude.

Just before we went into the front room for family prayer and the reading of the Christmas story, I overheard him say to somebody, "I don't know why Granddaddy keeps filling the children's heads full of that Santa Claus nonsense. I think it's ridiculous. If I had children, I wouldn't let him tell them all that junk."

I looked hard at Buford. I had never liked him, and I liked him even less now.

Our little daughter was so excited when Granddaddy started talking about "Sandy Claws" that she jumped up and down and clapped her hands.

When I took her up to bed, there was pure excitement in those big brown eyes. "Santa Claus is coming, Daddy! Santa Claus is coming, Daddy!"

I got a warm feeling all over, and I sure was glad to be back at Grandma's house at Christmastime.

After all the children had gone to sleep, the grown-ups started going out to their cars to get the toys they had brought for Santa Claus to leave under the Christmas tree.

I decided to wait until everybody else had finished before I put Dawn's presents out. This was a special time for me and I wanted to enjoy it.

After everybody had gone up to bed, I went to the car to get Dawn's toys. To my shock, I couldn't find them. I ran back into the house to my wife. "Sylvia, where did you pack Dawn's Christmas presents?"

"I thought you packed them."

I was close to panic, but I didn't want Sylvia to know it. I said, "Oh well, you just go on to bed, honey, and I'll look again. I probably just overlooked them."

I kissed my wife goodnight and went back downstairs.

I knew I hadn't overlooked them. We had somehow forgotten to pack them, and they were two thousand miles away in Denver, Colorado.

I was a miserable man. I just didn't feel like I could face little Dawn the next morning. She'd be so disappointed. All the other children would have the toys that Santa had brought them, and my beloved little daughter wouldn't have anything.

How could I have been so dumb? Here it was, twelve o'clock Christmas Eve night, all the stores closed, everybody in bed, and me without a single present for little Dawn. I was heartbroken. I went into the front room and sat by the dying fire, dejected and hopeless.

I don't know how long I sat there staring at the embers, but sometime later on I heard a rustle behind me and somebody said, "You got a match, son?"

I turned around and almost fell on the floor. Standing not ten feet from me was a short, fat little man in a red suit, with a long white beard and a pipe sticking out of his mouth.

I couldn't move, I couldn't speak. He looked at me and chuckled.

"Have you got a match, son? I ran out and I want to get this pipe going."

When I finally got my voice back, all I could say was, "Who are you?"

"Well, people call me by different names in different parts of the world, but around here they call me Santa Claus."

"No, I mean who are you really?"

"I just told you, son. How about that match?"

I stumbled to the mantelpiece, got a kitchen match, and gave it to him.

"Much obliged." He stood there lighting his pipe, with me looking at him like he was a ghost or something.

"How did you get in here?"

"Oh, I've got my ways."

"I thought you were supposed to slide down the chimney."

"That's a common misconception. Would you slide down a chimney with a fire at the bottom?"

"Well, no. I mean, no, sir."

"Well, neither would I."

"How did you get here?"

"I've got a sturdy sleigh and the finest team of reindeer a man could have."

"But we ain't got snow."

Santa Claus laughed so hard that his considerable belly shook. "I don't need snow. Half the places I go in the world don't have snow. Besides, I like to get out of the snow once in a while. We have it year-round at the North Pole, you know."

"You mean you really live at the North Pole?"

"Of course, I've always lived at the North Pole. Don't you know anything about Santa Claus, son?"

"Well, yeah, but I thought it was all a big put-on for the children."

"That's the trouble with you grown-ups. You think that everything you can't see is a put-on. It's a shame grown people can't be more like children. They don't have any trouble believing in me."

"You mean you've really got a sleigh, with reindeer named Donner and Blitzen and stuff like that?"

"That's right, son. There's Comet and Cupid and Donner and Blitzen and Dasher and Dancer and Prancer and Vixen. Of course, there's no Rudolph with the red nose. I don't know who came up with that one. Rudolph really is a put-on."

"But what are you doing here? Why did you come?"

"Because there's a little girl in this house who believes in me very much. Now, she'd be mighty disappointed to wake up Christmas morning and have nothing under the tree."

"You mean you came all the way here just because one little girl believes in you?"

"That's right, son. There's magic in believing. Besides, she's not the only one in this house who believes in me."

"Who else?"

"Why, your grandfather, of course."

"You mean Granddaddy wasn't putting us on all those years? He really believed in you?"

"Of course he believed in me."

"Well, why do you do this?"

"It's my way of celebrating the most important birthday in the history of man. Our Lord has given us so much. How can we do less?"

Santa Claus consulted a piece of paper he pulled out of his pocket and started taking a doll and other toys out of a big bag he had brought with him.

"Well, I've got to go, son. I've got a lot of stops to make before sunup. It's been really nice talking to you. Thanks for the match."

"Can I help you with your bag, Santa Claus?"

"No, that's all right, son. I'm used to carrying it."

I walked outside with him. "Where's your sleigh, Santa Claus?"

"It's parked right over there in the edge of the woods. You can come over and see it if you like." I started walking over to his sleigh with him, but then I had a thought.

"I'm gonna have to miss seeing your sleigh and reindeer. Thank you so very much. You saved my life. God bless you, Santa Claus. I'll see you next year."

"God bless you, too, son, and a Merry Christmas to you and yours."

Santa Claus started across the yard toward his sleigh, and I went running back in the house like a wild man. I raced up the stairs. "Buford, Buford, get up!"

"What's the matter, is the house on fire?"

"No, but hurry. Come out on the upstairs porch."

Buford grumbled as he got up and followed me out on the upstairs porch.

"What the heck do you want? It's cold out here."

"Just hush up and listen."

Well, we listened by a full minute and nothing happened.

"You're crazy. I'm going back to bed."

"Buford, if you go back in the house, you're gonna miss something that I want you, above all people, to see."

We waited for a little while longer and I had almost given up when I heard it. It was just a little tinkle at first, hanging on the frosty air and getting louder by the second. It was sleigh bells!

Buford looked at me and said, "Curtis, is this some kind of joke or something?"

"No, Buford, I swear it ain't. Just wait a minute now!"

The sound of sleigh bells was getting louder and Buford's face was getting whiter. "You got somebody out there doing that, ain't you? Admit it! You got somebody out there, ain't you?"

I didn't say a word. All of a sudden it sounded like somebody had flushed a covey of quail. That sleigh came up out of the woods and headed west, hovering just above the treetops.

Buford was speechless. I thought he was gonna pass out. He held on to the banister and took deep breaths.

Even if you believe so far, I know you ain't gonna believe this next part, but it really happened. Santa Claus made a big circle and turned and flew right around the house. I bet he won't over twenty feet from the upstairs porch when he passes by me and Buford. Old Santa Claus could really handle them reindeer. Then he headed west again, moving at a pretty good clip this time.

I hate to even tell you this next part, 'cause you'll think I took it right out of the book, but I didn't. Anyway, just about the time he was getting out of our hearing, he hollered, "Merry Christmas, everybody!"

And then he was gone.

"Curtis, do you know where Granddaddy keeps that bottle hid in the barn? I need me a drink."

I don't believe that Buford ever told anybody about seeing Santa Claus. I know I didn't, not until now. But I just had to tell somebody about it. It's been hard keeping it to myself all these years.

I'm a granddaddy myself now. That little girl that caused all this to happen with her faith in Santa Claus is grown and married and has a three-year-old girl and a five-year-old boy.

Me and Sylvia moved back to North Carolina many years ago and bought a big old farmhouse. Now my grandchildren come and spend Christmas with me and their grandmother. There's not as many of us as there was at Grandma's house, but we have just as big a time and celebrate Christmas just as hard.

In fact, Christmas is about the only time a year I'll take a drink. I always get me a pint of Old Granddad at Christmastime. Since the grandchildren are so small, I don't like to drink in front of them, so I keep my drinking whiskey hid out in the barn. When I want to go out there and get me a snort, I always tell the grandchildren that I've got to see if the cows got corn.

Of course, all the grown-ups know why I'm going out to the barn, or at least they think they do.

I always make my last trip to the barn after I've read the Christmas story and had family prayer. Everybody thinks I'm going out to get me a snort, but they're wrong.

I'm just going out to hear the sleigh bells ring.

CHRISTMAS THOUGHTS

Shortly after I've digested the Thanksgiving turkey and dressing and football games my thoughts start to stray toward my very favorite season of the year. The time of the year when we celebrate the birth of Jesus Christ, Christmas.

There are so many things that I love about Christmas that I couldn't possibly name them all, but I thought I'd put a few down.

- A fire in the fireplace and the smell of hardwood smoke.
- A Christmas tree loaded with shiny ornaments and just about as many bright-colored lights as it can hold.
- The cooking aromas coming out of Hazel's kitchen.
- Little kids coming down the stairs in soft down pajamas wiping the sleep from their eyes.
- Downtown Christmas decorations and the solitary beauty of a tree standing alone in someone's yard.
- "Chestnuts Roasting," "Silent Night," "White Christmas" and "Santa Claus Is Coming to Town."
- Heavy coats, gloves, and mufflers and seeing my breath in the air.
- Christmas carolers and department store Santa Clauses.
- Hearing someone say Merry Christmas.
- Watching a year-old child open a package, more interested in the wrapping paper than what's inside it.

- Cold silver moonlight shining through bare trees.
- Hot chocolate, eggnog and those little chicken salad sandwiches we always have before Christmas.
- Our employees' Christmas party where Santa Claus passes out gifts to about forty children.
- Calling all my employees' mothers on Christmas Eve day, something I've been doing for well over twenty years.
- Friends calling on the telephone just to wish you a Merry Christmas.
- Hearing about good things happening to needy people.
- "Frosty the Snowman," "Rudolph the Red Nosed Reindeer," and my very favorite, the Alastair Sim version of "A Dickens Christmas Carol."
- Holding Hazel's hand as we walk around and look at the decorations in our house.
- Reading St. Luke's Christmas story and a story I wrote to the friends and loved ones who gather at our house every Christmas Eve night.
- Watching the Midnight Mass from St. Peter's Basilica in Rome.
- Green wreaths with red ribbons, kind words, smiles and hugs, and children, children, children.
- Knowing that the Creator of the universe loves us enough to let His only son leave the unspeakable splendor of Heaven and the company of saints and angels and come to earth to be born in the humblest of circumstances in a barn in the company of barnyard animals.
- Remembering that once we get past the glitz and sparkle of Christmas that we are celebrating the greatest gift of all, Jesus Christ.

EVERY YEAR

Every year starting a day or so before Christmas I always get the feeling that there is something that I haven't done. I'm not referring to a forgotten gift for the family or some morsel of food or drink that I've forgotten to lay in.

No, I just always feel that I've overlooked some kindness, a remembrance to an old friend, a family in need, a toyless child, or a phone call to a sick person.

I always feel that I have not tried hard enough to identify need and loneliness, the ones without blankets or shelter.

The need is great and not always so visible, and I always feel that I should look a little more diligently. Christmas truly is a season of good will and giving, commemorating the greatest gift of all, the gift of free salvation given to all mankind by almighty God through his only begotten son, Jesus. So I guess it's natural to feel more sensitive toward the needs of others at that special time of year.

But if you stop and think about it, Jesus didn't just give during the Christmas season. The gift which he gave is truly the gift that keeps on giving, 365 days a year and 366 on leap year, twenty-four hours a day.

The gift He gives does not wear out, decay, nor get used up. This gift is designed to last not a lifetime, but throughout eternity.

Every year when it becomes time for New Year's resolutions I inevitably resolve to be a better Christian only to find myself stumbling and falling all year long, never becoming the person that I really desire to be, but God never repossesses my gift, He just forgives me and picks me up, even knowing that I'll stumble again, maybe before the day is even over. Oh, what a wonderful God we serve!

Imperfect person that I am, I have discovered that there is one perfect thing that we can do. Simply to love each other. And not just the successful, beautiful people in our lives, not just the ones who can be beneficial to us in some way, not just our friends and family members.

We must love the needy, the addicted, the obnoxious, and the haughty. We must remember Jesus died for everyone, not just the few, but for everybody who was ever born on this planet.

Sometimes real love is hard to practice because we want to strike back at the ones who strike out at us, we want to reserve the right to criticize and chastise.

Well, my New Year's resolution this year will be a little different. It still has to do with being a better Christian, but I will endeavor in 2000 to be a kinder, more understanding person. I resolve to extend courtesies to everyone I come into contact with.

I will not be unkind to the harried airline employee when the flight's running late.

I will be more patient with someone who's having a bad day.

I will try to be more sympathetic to people who have problems in their lives.

I will try to be more sensitive to the needs of others.

I will stand against things such as abortion and the taking away of our rights.

I will speak the truth to the best of my knowledge.

I know that I will again stumble and fall in the coming year, but I'm hoping that next year when Christmas rolls around I won't feel as if I've left so much undone.

Happy New Year, everybody.